Sarah Ōtagawa

EASY BENTO COOKBOOK

365 DAYS OF TRADITIONAL JAPANESE LUNCHBOX RECIPES

TABLE of CONTENTS

INTRODUCTION
To The Bento Cookbook

BENTO, JAPANESE CUISINE MADE SIMPLE

Japanese cuisine is recognized for its seasonal celebrations, notably in the form of seasonal ingredients. Washoku, Japan's officially designated national cuisine, is known for its use of locally sourced, seasonal ingredients.

Aside from the fact that the food in Japanese meals is delicious, it is frequently remarked that they are also a visual treat; since each dish is designed to highlight the cuisine, it contains and is sometimes adorned with a seasonal flower or leaf. As the diner eats, their eyes feast momentarily on the food, leaving just the recollection of what it looked like & the sensual delight of having eaten it.

TO a Japanese's eye westerners tend to over-confuse the components in their food, going often overboard by mashing all kinds of different tastes in their different cuisines. This cannot be said of Japanese food. The Washoku is founded instead on a belief that simplification is the most important ingredient in their food. Using only fresh & seasonal ingredients, Japanese cuisine creates a reverence for the food. Because they are working with these fresh ingredients, chefs try to do as small as necessary to alter the food's appearance or flavor.
There is no doubt that the quality of the components is a big part of the solution. Small, elegantly presented meals and the modest approach to the products used & simple cooking methods wherever feasible contribute to a compelling gastronomic voyage, not to mention the restriction of overbearing flavors. Even if Japanese cuisine is very complex, one thing is certain: there are reasons that people from all over the globe visit exquisite Japanese restaurants daily. Japanese cuisine has a unique ability to satisfy our senses, leave a lasting impression, and keep us going back for more!

The reasons to be enamored with Japanese cuisine are plenty. First, it's good for you! Healthy vitamins aren't destroyed when food is prepared healthily by steaming, stewing, simmering, boiling, or frying with little or no oil. Many components are beneficial to one's health, such as natto, which aids digestion, and shiitake mushrooms, which help fight cancer. Buckwheat-based soba noodles & sashimi (finely diced raw fish served over rice) are two further examples of foods good for protein, cholesterol, and omega-3 fatty acids.

Appreciate your bento's flavor and savor the moment. Cultivate a passion for beautiful things in life.

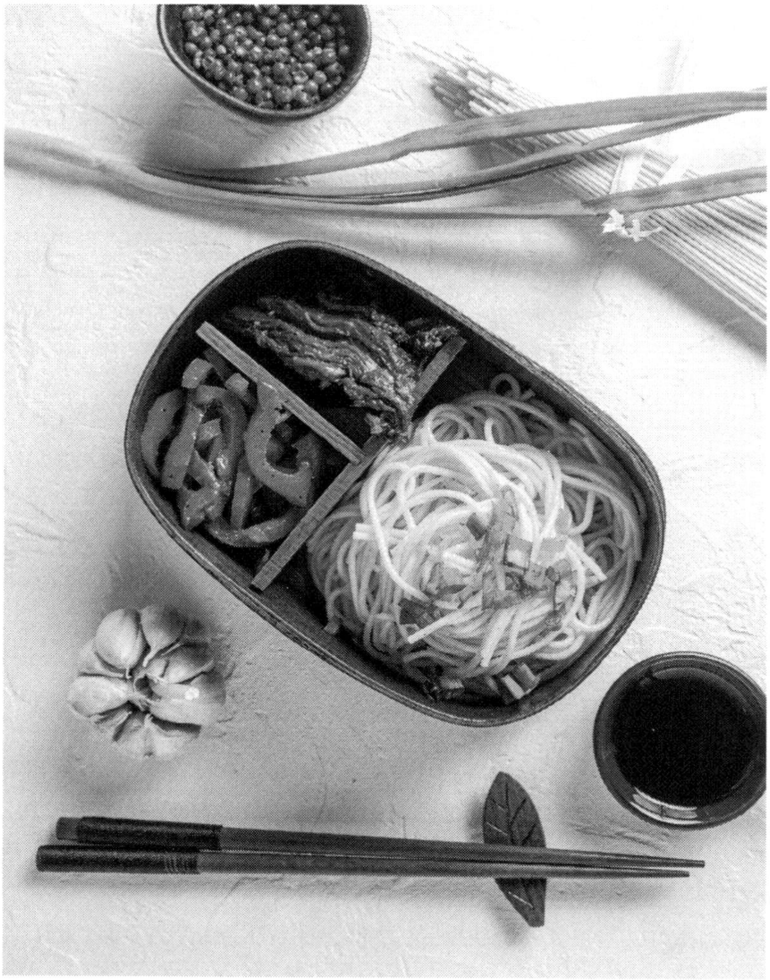

To counterbalance the yin & yang energies, you may find sweeter meals alongside saltier ones or hot dishes that are both sour and salty. Everything here revolves on deceiving your sense of taste! It's a great way to keep things fresh while still getting the greatest health advantages.

Those interested in Japanese cuisine may find this series of books useful. In this book we will focus on one of the most traditional and socially important way (philosophy?) of eating: the Bento box lunch.

Traditionally, a bento is a compact, flat box with dividers filled with a classic box lunch. It consists of meat, fish, rice, and vegetables in modest servings. Take-out bento boxes are available at convenience stores, and some include Western-style foods like sausages and pasta. This Japanese rice ball dish is popular among teenagers and adults. ***Let't take a look right away of four of the most frequent kind of traditional food you can find inside a bento box.***

BASIC TRADITIONAL BENTO RECIEPES

Gohan (Boiled Rice)

Rice is traditionally eaten with the left hand, near to the lips, serving four people. Rice is pushed into the mouth with chopsticks as the bowl is gently turned in the hands.

Ingredients

- 1 cup of Japanese uncooked short-grain rice (available at the majority of supermarkets & Asian food retailers)
- 1 & ¼ cups of water

Procedure

1. Set aside around 30 mins to soak the rice before draining it.
2. Bring the rice and water back to a boil in the same pot and remove them from the heat.
3. Reduce the heat, cover, & simmer for another 15 mins or more, unless the rice has absorbed all of the water, then remove from the fire.
4. Keep the lid on and let the rice steam for approximately 15 mins on medium heat.
5. Chopsticks are required for serving (optional).

RICE BALL (ONIGIRI)

Ingredients – Serves 10|12.

- 2 cups of rice cooked
- Salt
- Pickled plums, sliced into tiny, bite-sized slices
- Cooked salmon, sliced into tiny, bite-sized slices
- sheets (nori) Dry seaweed, chopped into slices

Procedure

1. Rice should be cooked according to the package's instructions. Allow to cool down a little.
2. The water should be at room temperature.
3. Sprinkle salt over wet hands after dipping them in clean water.
4. Put a tiny pile of rice (approximately 2 Tbsp).
5. Cooked salmon or a pickled plum may be inserted into the mound.
6. To produce a triangle mound, twirl your mound back & forth among wet, salty palms.
7. Wrap the mound with a piece of dried seaweed.
8. Chopsticks are required for serving (optional).

CHICKEN TERIYAKI

Ingredients – Serves 6

½ cup of soy sauce (Japanese style)

- 3 tbsp sugar
- 1 tbsp grated fresh ginger root
- 3 tbsp seeds sesame
- 1 & ½ - 2 lb chicken breast skinless, boneless, sliced into tiny serving pieces

Procedure

1. Preheat the oven to 375 degrees Fahrenheit.
2. Combine the sugar, ginger, soy sauce, & sesame seeds.
3. Pour the sauce over the chicken before roasting it.
4. Cook 45 mins of baking time. As you rotate the chicken, slather it with sauce as you go along.

PEANUT MOCHI SWEET (RICE CAKES)

Rice cakes are a traditional New Year's Eve and Children's Day dessert option. Asian markets and specialty grocery shops may sometimes carry these items.

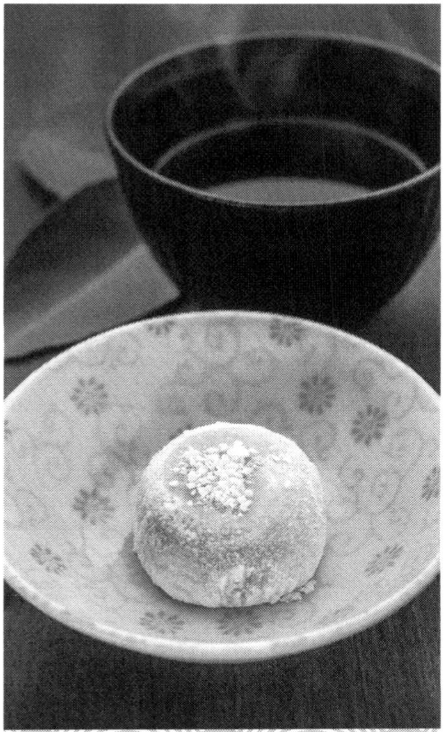

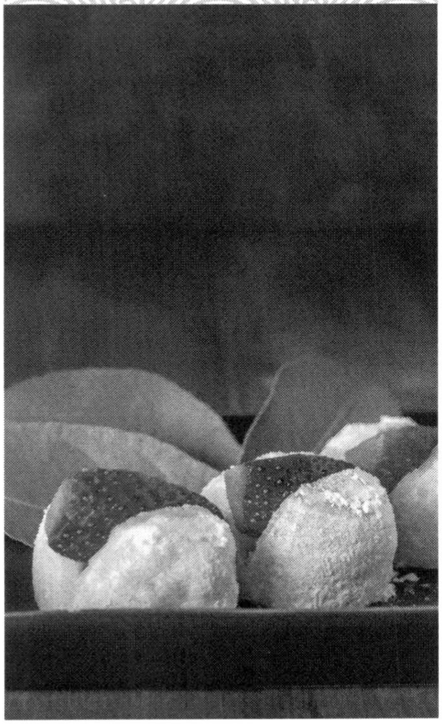

Ingredients

- 1 cup of glutinous-rice sweet flour (mochiko)
- ¼ tsp of salt
- ¼ cup of light brown packed sugar
- ½ cup of unsalted cocktail peanuts
- ½ cup of water
- cornstarch or Potato starch
- rice syrup, molasses, or blossom orange honey
- ½ cup optional soybean powder roasted kinako)

Procedure

1. For around 30 seconds, gently knead the dough.
2. Bring Four cups of water to a rolling boil in a large saucepan or wok.
3. Cover the steamer tray with a wet piece of cheesecloth or unbleached muslin.
4. A 12-inch-thick layer of dough should be spread out evenly across the fabric.
5. Place your steamer on the simmering water in the saucepan. Twenty mins of steaming under a cover.
6. Lift the dough-covered cloth from the pan & remove it from the tray.
7. Remove the cloth, allowing the dough to fall onto a floured surface. Cool for 2 mins.
8. Knead for about a min or until the dough is silky and glossy. Slice the 8" long sausage roll into Eight equal pieces.
9. To keep things from sticking, sprinkle a little cornstarch on top. Create smooth, circular forms by forming them Roll rice cakes in soybean powder & drizzle honey over them.
10. Serve with teacups of warm green tea on individual plates. Wrap the mound with a piece of dried seaweed.

THE BENEFITS OF EATING TRADITIONAL JAPANESE CUISINE

Fish, seafood, & plant-based meals are the mainstays of a traditional Japanese diet, low in animal protein, refined carbohydrates, and saturated fat. This meal is influenced by the "washoku" style of Japanese cooking, consisting of tiny plates of seasonal, locally sourced foodstuffs.Many health advantages may be gained by following this diet, including weight reduction, better digestion, and general well-being.

Everything you require to understand the Japanese diet may be found here.

WHAT IS THE TRADITIONAL JAPANESE DIET?

Seasonal, lightly processed foods are offered in tiny servings in the traditional Japanese diet. Instead of relying on sauces or condiments to conceal the taste of a meal, this kind of eating enhances its inherent flavor.

Rather than relying on processed foods, the diet relies on natural carbohydrates and fats like steamed or stir-fried rice, noodles, fish, and tofu. The recipe may also include a tiny amount of dairy, eggs, or meat. More rice and fish may be found in traditional Japanese cuisine than in Okinawan cuisine, which originated on Okinawa Japanese island. The significant Western & Chinese influences of this way of cooking differ from the current Japanese diet, characterized by a greater emphasis on animal protein & processed foods.

Fresh, locally sourced, and seasonally prepared meals make up a large part of traditional Japanese cuisine. Small quantities of sugar, lipids & animal protein are included, but the emphasis is on seafood, fish, rice, noodles, seaweed & soy products.

BENTO BOX HISTORY

Bento is very popular Japanese version of a take out, or home-packed meal, usually consumed at lunch. The term Bento comes from the Chinese, biandang, and its meaning - convenient - hides a property that makes it one of the most used habits for millions of people every single day.

If you're a fan of anime and manga I'm sure you have seen several times your favorite characters enjoying their meals in bento boxes. They are deeply rooted in Japanese daily lives. Many children bring bentos made by their parents in the morning to schools.

The simplicity of Bento's concept has been appreciated for a long long time in Japanese cooking - and eating - culture. In fact, Bento is 10 century old!

The historians traced the earliest version of Bento back to the Kamakura period (1185 - 1333) when it was very common for people to cook their own rice and carrying it in small bags to work.

The origin of bentos as we know them today raised during the latter half of the Sengoku era (1467 - 1615), when they were luxurious entertainment for upper class people, when they desired to enjoy meals outside for Hanami (spring blossoming) or the autumn leaves falling. They were originally called Sagju, and were often enjoyed alongside a good bottle of Sake. The boxes themselves were a work of art, de-

stined to make nobles enjoy not only the food, but also the beauty of nature with all of their 5 senses. During the peaceful Edo era (1603 - 1868) Bento have also always been used to have meals while watching stage art. As entertainment became gradually a custom for all so did bentos. Imagine the joy of Japanese families enjoying their bento meal during the break of a Kabuki show.

Bento followed the evolution and the progression of Japanese society. Another example is what is probably the most famous of bentos, the ekiben: as railways became common this kind of bento was to be found everywhere in stations and aboard trains.
Each region used special ingredients to make their local cuisine and as a way to promote their cities and attracts tourists. After WW2 Japan experienced a rapid economic growth and Bento boxes started to be sold everywhere in Japan, from convenience store to grocery store and became ordinary for everyone to buy and eat at home.

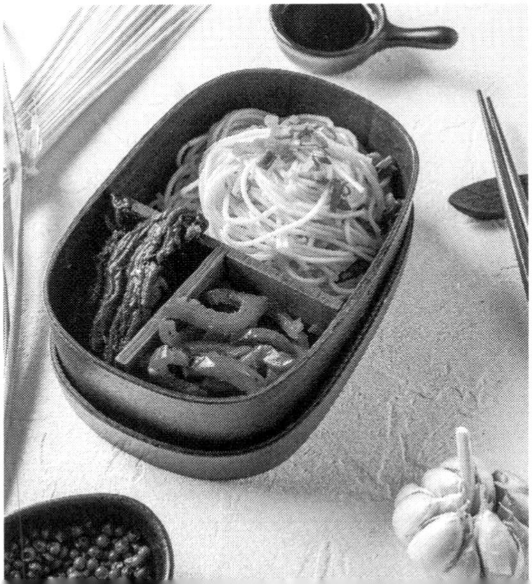

Bentos became soon traditional for kids as families had to provide food to bring for the lunch at school. They soon lost their centrality as school meals though, as schools started to provide lunches for students. It regained new popularity in the 80's due to the wide commercialization of microwave ovens.

Today school meals are provided at certain schools in Japan; however, some schools still require pupils to bring their lunch from home. Nowadays the most common and popular Bento is the Kyaraben, abbreviation of character-bento, made and arranged so that they look like cute and beautifully designed animals and anime characters. Usually made by parents for their kids to take to school they have become a photographable item that often turns in a trend in children and teenagers' social circles. The more effort parents put in making their kid's bento, the better parent they are... in a kind of untold rule of social showing off. People eat bento during school, at work, during picnics or flower-viewing, as food at home, or as part of huge group events. In addition to children, many adults bring their bento boxes to work. Some individuals like to have their bento prepared for them by their parents or spouses, while others prefer to create their own. When a loved one prepares a bento for you to eat, you're sure to feel a great connection to them. Making and eating bento may be a way to communicate with one another.

BENTO ON THE TRAIN

Bentos are so popular and practical that a specific type of these boxed meals are sold at a large quantity in trains and at trains station in Japan. The ekiben is to these days one of the most widely-used because they offer a complete and balanced meal to any Japanese worker who wants to purchase his or her meal on the way to work instead of preparing it at home.
Meiji-era ekiben have been historically offered at railway stations, & there are currently 2-3 thousand variations of ekiben on the market in Japan, with sushi bento, makunouchi bento, and bento packed with local flavor striving to deliver the greatest taste. Bidders would use a box worn around the neck to queue for passengers on the platforms and then sell the boxes to those on board the trains when they came to a halt. Bullet trains and restricted express trains have seen a rise in non-opening windows as the railroad industry has evolved, and now travelers in Japan may still buy ekiben from shops on platforms or from the food carts roaming inside trains, even if they can no longer do so via the window when their trains are halted.

In addition to specialty bento shops, you can now buy bento in various venues, including supermarkets, convenience stores, and department stores. People may find a wide range of bento, including Chinese-style and Western-style bento, the traditional makunouchi and seaweed Bento. The convenience of taking home the delicacies cooked by restaurant chefs in the comfort of one's house is now made possible by restaurants, not simply those providing Japanese cuisine.

THE BENTO BOX

A Bento box is a container designed to contain one meal per one person. It usually contains one serving or rice and 1 to 4 spaces more for side dishes. Today it is very usual to consume a bento in a plastic box, but you can also find and purchase a fancier traditional box like:

Wooden Bento: Nothing beats the warm look and feel of a handmade bento box made out of bent sheets of wood. It's a compact and resistant box that is not thought to use for frequent washing or microwave use, but more conceived as a piece of art made by an artisan. It is usually curved and oval in shape and it's typical of the Yayoi period (10th to 3rd century BC). The interior was designed for absolute simplicity with a wooden divider at one third of the box length creating just 2 spaces (tiers) in the box.

Bamboo Bento: Those charming boxes are made out of weaved allow or bamboo. This kind of box is optimal for maintaining tastes, but not adapt for any food in liquid form.

Half Moon Bento: This elegant piece is a half moon shaped bento box said to be the favorite of Sen no Rikyu, known as the highest master of the way of tea ceremony in late 16th century. If you can get your hands on one of this bentos keep it dearly.

BPA-free Plastic Bento: these are the most common and most practical bento boxes perfect for every-day use. Mosto of them are dishwasher and microwave safe. Reasonably priced and come in all kinds of designs and colors. If you're a beginner in the Bento's world, I suggest you to start from this very practical box; you'd be surprised to find out how lovely some of them are.

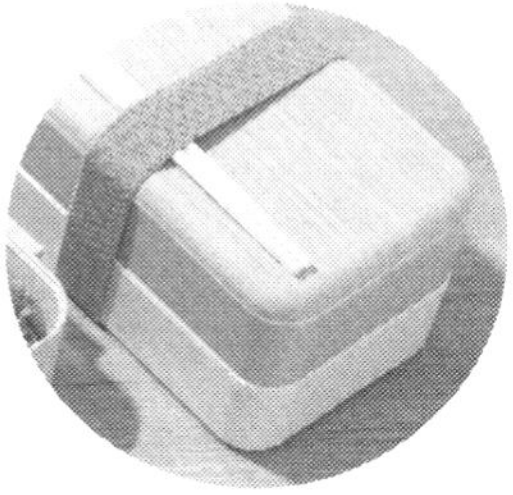

The perfect Bento Box should posses the following qualities:

LEAKPROOF

Especially if you're just starting out, the container should be as leakproof as possible. The one thing you don't want is your container to be leaking liquids. If the box is not made out of plastic, look for those with leak resistant rubber seals. You can do a leak test by filling the box with water and shaking it a little bit. Check for moistures around the edges.

MICROVAWE-FRIENDLY

You may probably want to heat your bento or the leftovers of a bento at a later time, so make sure to get a box that has no problem to be heated in a microwave oven. Microwave-friendly boxes are useful if you want to heat a refrigerated bento lunch: bentos are meant to be eaten at room temperature.

EASY TO WASH

The Box should be easy to wash. Most boxes are not dishwasher safe, so if you don't plan to handwash your box, you may want to get one that can be safely placed and washed in a dishwasher.

BENTO SIZE

Now you may ask: how big should be a Bento and how much food should it contain?
Well, the answer is... it depends. The real question should be: how big is your appetite? You can refer to the general guide below which shows suggested bento capacity (400mL to 900mL) based on two factors: age and appetite. People with more sedentary lifestyles should subtract 100mL from these suggested bento sizes, while those with an active lifestyles can add on 100mL.

AGE	LARGE APPETITE	SMALL APPETITE
3-5 years	400ml	400ml
6-8 years	500ml	500ml
9-11 years	600ml	600ml
12-20 years	900ml	700ml
20-40 years	900ml	600ml
50-60 years	800ml	600ml
70 years	600ml	500ml

THE BALANCED BENTO

The Bento lunch has become widely popular throughout Japanese history because it permitted workers to control their food intake in an easy way, by eating a healthy and balanced diet.

As bentos come in compartmentalized containers, it's very easy to control and have a good estimate of the amount of food you will eat in one meal.

In a perfectly balanced bento you will find:

CARBS

rice, yakisoba, yaki udon, takikomi gohan.
The first step is to put carbs. Carbs are a very important source of energy and should make a consistent part of your box. In a 2 compartment box, half should be filled with a rice based recipes (you will find many options in this book).

PROTEINS

Meat, fish, and seafood (karaage, gyoza, teriyaki salmon)

SIDES

tofu, egg, or mushroom dishes, hijiki salad, potato salad, tamagoyaki, green bean gomaae, kinpira renkon

FRUIT

the most used are berries, grapes, apples. Fruit can be placed inside the box or also in a separate container.

FILLERS

simple yet colorful ingredients to brighten the bento (like boiled egg, blanched broccoli or cherry tomatoes)

COLORS MATTER!

> If you love bentos, there's no way around it: you've got to love the way they look. When in doubt on which food to fill your bentos with, always go with bold colors to maximize visual impact!
> One untold rule of bentos says that every bento should contain the colors red or orange, yellow, green, white and black. With this colors you can make sure your bento will look like if you've just ordered it from a Japanese local store! Beside looking great, colorful vegetables and fruits are often high in nutrients.

If you love bentos, there's no way around it: you've got to love the way they look. When in doubt on which food to fill your bentos with, always go with bold colors to maximize visual impact!
One untold rule of bentos says that every bento should contain the colors red or orange, yellow, green, white and black. With this colors you can make sure your bento will look like if you've just ordered it from a Japanese local store! Beside looking great, colorful vegetables and fruits are often high in nutrients.

If you have two colorful vegetables, like asparagus and broccoli, separate them by positioning them on the sides and place other food between them to make the bento more symmetric and visually appealing. With experience you will learn to make your bentos look like real Japanese ones!
The most vivid and liveliest of the colors is RED: use tomatoes, bell peppers, strawberries, raspberries, red radish and apples to add some red to the lunch. For a sunny YELLOW/ORANGE splash you can add oranges, lemons, bananas, pumpkins, sweet potatoes or corn. Use lettuce, kiwis, edamame, asparagus, parsley, Brussel sprouts, green onions or cucumber if you want a GREEN overall look in your box. If instead you need to tone down the brighter colors a bit for contrast, you can use WHITE/BLACK/BROWN food like shiitake mushrooms, onions, daikon radish, nori seaweed, or sesame seeds.

PACK YOUR BENTO

Bento's preparation, once the food is ready, cooked, or refrigerated is quite a daily ritual tradition for many people of Japan.
First, and most importantly, place your carbs source, Generally the biggest tier is used to host carbs as energy is of the ut-most importance for what the bentos were conceived for, os your rice can be placed here to give a wide white space to the box.
Second, place some healthy protein close to the rice, and usually shouldn't use more than 1/4 of the whole box. If you can add two different kinds of proteins.
Add sides (usually a vegetable) to another 1/4 tier and fill the missing spaces with whatever filling you need or is required.
One of the most important action you can take while preparing a bento is to pack the different foods in a tight manner, to prevent food from moving around and screw the order. Also, remember to remove any liquid from food, unless you have a box that allows you to do so.
In this book you will find plenty of recipes ideas with which you can pack thousands of different bentos. Remember, variety is key! With the recipes you're going to read in this book you will be ready to have enough combinations to eat 365 days of bento! Enjoy!

TAMAGOYAKI / ROLLED OMELETTE

Preparation — **5 MIN**

Cooking — **5 MIN**

Servings — **2**

INGREDIENTS

- Eggs 4 large
- 3 tbsp. of soup of stock dashi
- 2 tbsps. of sugar
- Vegetable oil, as wanted

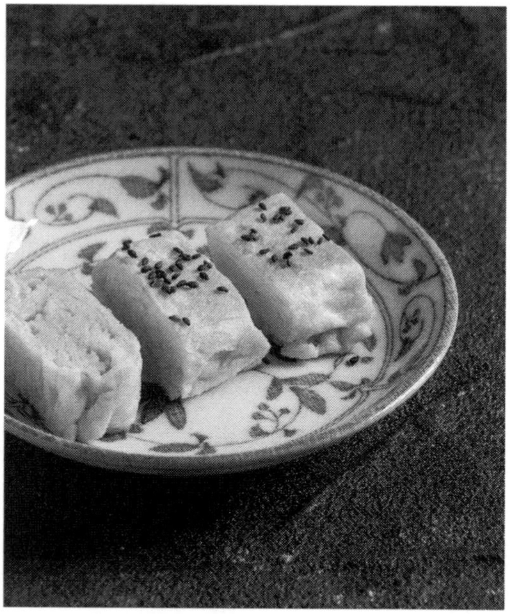

NUTRITION

Calories 255 Kcal | Carbohydrate 13g
fat 16 g
Protein 13 g

INSTRUCTIONS

1. Collect the ingredients carefully. In a separate dish, whisk the eggs until they are light and fluffy.
2. Sugar and dashi soup should be mixed well into the egg. Add water to the tamagoyaki pan and bring it to a boil over medium-high heat. Apply some vegetable oil to the pan. A spoonful of the egg mixture should be added to the pan and then spread out to cover the whole pan surface.
3. When the egg is half-cooked, turn it over and roll it towards the bottom. The rolled egg should now be on the other side.
4. Pour the spoonful of egg mixture over the rolled egg and into the empty area in the pan, which has been oiled.
5. The thicker the omelet, the longer it takes to cook, so cook it until it's about halfway done. It is done when the omelet has reached the desired doneness in the pan.
6. Arrange tamagoyaki on the bamboo mat using a standard frying pan. If you're using a standard pan, form it on a bamboo mat. Tamagoyaki should be cut into 1" thick slices.
7. Serve it for breakfast, as a side dish in a bento box, or as a sushi filler.

JAPANESE RICE BALLS

Preparation — **5 MIN**

Cooking — **30 MIN**

Servings — **6-8**

INGREDIENTS

- 2 sheets of nori seaweed, dried
- 4 cups of Japanese rice, steamed
- Kosher salt, for taste
- For the Fillings:
- 1 umeboshi
- 1 salmon fillet

NUTRITION

Calories 119 Kcal | fat 1 g |
Carbohydrate 25 g|
Protein 2 g

INSTRUCTIONS

1. Collect the ingredients. Prepare a dish of steamed rice with half a cup of nori sheets (if using).
2. To prevent the rice from sticking to your hands, wet them with water. Your damp hands will benefit from a little salt.
3. Make a triangle out of steamed rice in your hands, ensuring it's dense and heavy.
4. Whether grilled salmon or umeboshi, rice may be topped with any filling.
5. Raise the rice with your hands. Press softly to shape the rice into a circle, triangle, or cylinder and secure the filling in the center. Lightly push the rice ball as you roll it around in your palms.
6. Wrap the rice balls with nori (if using) or sprinkle sesame seeds on these if you'd like (if using).

TERIYAKI CHICKEN BENTO

Preparation — **20 MIN**

Cooking — **15 MIN**

Servings — **2**

INGREDIENTS

- 3/4 pound of boneless chicken thighs
- 4 tbsps. of soy sauce
- 4 tbsps. of mirin
- 2 tbsps. of sake
- 2 tbsps. of sugar
- 1 pinch of fresh ginger, grated
- 2 tsp. of olive oil

NUTRITION

Calories 561 Kcal | fat 28 g |
Carbohydrate 29 g|
Protein 43 g

INSTRUCTIONS

1. Collect the ingredients. To further absorb the teriyaki sauce's flavors, poke the chicken with a fork while it cooks.
2. Prepare teriyaki sauce first. Mirin, Soy sauce, sake and sugar are all mixed in a big bowl.
3. Add the olive oil to a large pan and heat it over medium heat. Place them skin-side down a chicken in the pan and cook it until it's browned and crispy.
4. Turn down your stove's heat to low and flip the chicken over to fry the other side.
5. Toss chicken in the pan with the teriyaki sauce used to marinade it. Cook chicken over low heat with the lid on until it reaches an interior temperature of 165 degrees Fahrenheit, and the juices flow clear.
6. Remove the top and let the sauce boil for a few minutes until it thickens. Then, turn off the stovetop and let the pan cool.
7. Cut the chicken, then serve it on a dish. " It is now time to drizzle some of the sauce on top of the chicken breasts.
8. Decorate teriyaki chicken with more grated ginger if you choose.

JAPANESE BUNNY APPLE SNACKS

Preparation — **10 MIN**

Cooking — **0 MIN**

Servings — **2**

INGREDIENTS

- 4 medium-size apples

INSTRUCTIONS

1. Slice Apple into Small Slices. Cut every apple into six to eight wedges before eating. If you keep an apple wedge on hand, you may utilize it for this task. Every apple slice should have its core removed. This step may be omitted if you wedged your apple using an apple wedge.

2. Slice apple in inverted V forms using a knife and delicately remove the apple's peel with the blade.

3. Take off the apple's triangular part. Avoid browning your apple bunnies by soaking them for several mins in saltwater before using them.

4. Apple rabbits make a delicious dessert or a tasty addition to bento lunches. Whether you want to serve them with peanut butter or the other dip, it's up to you.

NUTRITION

Calories 52 Kcal | fat 0.2 g |
Carbohydrate 13 g|
Protein 0.3 g

SHOYU TAMAGO / SOY SAUCE EGGS

Preparation — **5 MIN**

Cooking — **5 MIN**

Servings — **4**

INGREDIENTS

- 4 large, hard-boiled eggs
- 5 tbsps. of soy sauce

INSTRUCTIONS

1. Gather the necessary items for the recipe. Boil eggs and remove the shells. Using water, make sure you get rid of any stray shell pieces you may have.
2. Remove from consideration. Put soy sauce to a boil in a small saucepan. Remove the pan from heat and stir in the cooked, peeled eggs. Gently roll eggs in soy sauce and mix with a rubber spatula so that eggs don't get nicked.
3. For a mildly salty taste, steep eggs in the soy sauce for 2 minutes; for a more pronounced flavour, soak eggs for 5 minutes. Prepare the food and serve it to your guests.

NUTRITION

Calories 82 Kcal | fat 5 g |
Carbohydrate 1 g|
Protein 8 g

TSUKUNE / JAPANESE MEATBALLS

Preparation — **15 MIN**

Cooking — **20 MIN**

Servings — **5**

INGREDIENTS

- 1 pound of ground chicken
- 1 egg
- 2 tbsps. of sliced scallions
- 1 tbsp of diced onion
- 1 tbsp of cornstarch
- 1 tbsp of miso paste
- 1 tsp of grated ginger
- 1 tsp of soy sauce
- 1/2 tsp of salt

For the Sauce:

- 1/2 cup of soy sauce
- 1/2 cup of mirin
- 2 tbsps. of brown sugar
- 1 tsp of cornstarch
- 1 tsp of grated garlic
- 1 tsp. of grated ginger
- garnish scallions
- garnish lime wedges

NUTRITION

Calories 310 Kcal | fat 11 g |
Carbohydrate 26 g|
Protein 26 g

INSTRUCTIONS

1. Boil a significant amount of water. Blend all ingredients until they're finely minced. The onions with scallions should be cut into tiny pieces.
2. Scoop out a little amount of meat mixture using a cookie scoop and set aside. To avoid dumping too much meat into the pot, keep the edges of the scoop clean.
3. Drop the meat combination into boiling liquid. Eventually, you'll be able to prepare four or five meals at once. Cook for around three mins. They would be grilled again, so don't worry if the insides are still raw.
4. Remove those from boiling water with a slotted spoon and arrange them on the serving dish. You should be able to skewer around 3 meatballs over each, based on the size of every piece.
5. Make the Sauce and Grill the Meatballs
6. The following ingredients should be combined in a small saucepan: soy sauce; brown sugar; mirin; cornstarch; garlic; plus, ginger. Stirring often, cooking for 5 mins or till thickened over medium heat is the way to go here.
7. Grill a steak on a hot grill pan. The pan should be sprayed using cooking spray before use. Using a grill pan, heat skewers of meatballs in the pan for 2 mins. As the meat is cooking, coat it with sauce. Then turn and cook on the other side for yet another minute, brushing sauce on the other side.
8. Immediately remove from grill & serve with more sticky sauce, scallions, and lime juice.

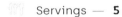

HOT DOG OCTOPUS

Preparation — **3 MIN**

Cooking — **1 MIN**

Servings — **1**

INGREDIENTS

- one hot dog

INSTRUCTIONS

1. Gather the necessary items for the recipe. Discard the ends of the hot dog after cutting it in half horizontally.
2. Afterward, slice the hot dog in halves horizontally, leaving the two-inch portion linked at the end. As of this point, the octopus should have 4 legs.
3. Split each of the four legs into two halves. It is when a sharp knife comes in handy since the legs of certain hot dogs might be thin and delicate.
4. Spread legs of hot dog out on a microwave-safe platter. Use a high-powered microwave for 30-40 secs. During this process, you might expect your arms to get curly & your head to swell in size. Be careful to stretch out hot dogs' legs before cooking in a steamer basket to cook evenly.

NUTRITION

Calories 180 |fat 3 g |
Carbohydrate 24 g |
Protein 20 g

POTATO KOROKKE

Preparation — **30 MIN**

Cooking — **15 MIN**

Servings — **5**

INGREDIENTS

- 4 peeled with quartered medium potatoes
- 2 cups of vegetable oil
- 1/4 pound of ground beef
- 1/2 finely chopped medium onion
- salt, for taste
- Black pepper freshly ground for taste
- 1/4 cup of flour
- 1 egg large, beaten
- 1 cup of panko breadcrumbs
- Tonkatsu sauce, used for serving

NUTRITION

Calories 556 Kcal | fat 26 g |
Carbohydrate 63 g|
Protein 18 g

INSTRUCTIONS

1. Gather the necessary items for the recipe. Boil a medium-sized kettle of water. Using a potato peeler, peel and quarter potatoes. When a skewer easily passes through them, they're ready to serve.
2. In a colander, drain & return potatoes to a saucepan. While potatoes are still warm, use a potato masher to mash them.
3. Sauté beef with onion in some oil in a medium-sized pan till the meat is no longer pink in the middle.
4. Cooked meat and onion should be mixed with mashed potatoes. Salt & pepper to taste, then allow the mix to cool before serving.
5. Flatten the ingredients into oval patties using your hands when it has cooled.
6. In a heavy-bottomed saucepan, heat oil to 350 degrees Fahrenheit.
7. Using three shallow bowls (one for each of the three ingredients), mix beaten egg, flour, and panko breadcrumbs until they form a smooth paste. Sprinkle flour over every potato patty before cooking. To remove any excess, drop in the beaten egg & allow it to drain. To finish, sprinkle on the panko.
8. Fry till golden brown & crispy, turning as necessary, in the batches if necessary. Avoid overcrowding the pot. Proceed to drain the rest of korokke in the same manner.
9. Serve with a sauce of your choice.

SPINACH AND BEAN SPROUT NAMUL

Preparation — **13 MIN**

Cooking — **2 MIN**

Servings — **2**

INGREDIENTS

- 6 oz of spinach
- 9 oz of bean sprout
- ¼ tsp of sea salt

Seasonings (make it for each ingredient)

- 1 Tbsp of sesame oil, roasted
- ½ tsp of sea salt
- 1 garlic clove

NUTRITION

Calories 131 Kcal | fat 8 g |
Carbohydrate 13 g|
Protein 7 g

INSTRUCTIONS

BEAN SPROUT NAMUL

1. Removing the brown sections with stringy roots enhances the flavour of bean sprouts, particularly when they are seasoned simply.
2. Mix 1 Tablespoon sesame oil, half tsp salt, and 1 minced garlic clove in a medium mixing bowl.
3. Cut up a chili pepper & remove the seeds before chopping them into tiny chunks. If you wish it hot, you may keep seeds there as a garnish.
4. A big saucepan of water should be brought to a boil. Add 1/4 teaspoon of salt plus the bean sprouts to the boiling water.
5. Using a fine-mesh sieve or skimmer, remove any bean sprouts that have formed. Get rid of all the water. Keep water if you're also making Spinach Namul.
6. At a minimum, an hour before serving, coat bean sprouts with spices & transfer them to a meal prep bowl with a cover. The bean sprout may be refrigerated for four days.

SPINACH NAMUL

7. Add 1 Tablespoon sesame oil, 1/2 teaspoon salt, and 1 minced garlic clove to the medium bowl and mix.
8. Maintaining stems on the bottom with leaves above, hold spinach upright. At the same time, hold leaves, and blanch the stem for 15 secs. Cooking from the stem end first takes a little

longer since the stem takes longer to cook. After that, cook for further 30-45 seconds with the leaves immersed in the pan.

9. After draining, rinse the spinach in icy water to halt the cooking process. Drain spinach, then run it under the icy water to chill it down.
10. Squeeze the water out of the spinach before storing it. Add spinach plus spices to the bowl and toss to combine. Cut spinach into 1-inch pieces.
11. Let it marinate for at minimum an hour after serving after combining all the ingredients. Refrigerated spinach keeps for up to five days.

QUICK BENTO: SAUTEED SPINACH

Preparation — **5 MIN**

Cooking — **5 MIN**

Servings — **1**

INGREDIENTS

- 1 Tbsp of unsalted butter
- spinach
- canned of frozen corn
- Sea salt or kosher
- black pepper, freshly ground

INSTRUCTIONS

1. Melt the butter in a pan over medium heat.
2. Sauté the spinach with corn, both frozen, till they are warm.
3. Remove the food from the oven and serve it immediately.

NUTRITION

Calories 158 Kcal | fat 7 g |
Carbohydrate 19 g|
Protein 11 g

NIKUJAGA / MEAT & POTATO STEW

Preparation — **15 MIN**

Cooking — **15 MIN**

Servings — **4**

INGREDIENTS

- 1 onion
- 1 carrot
- 3 Yukon of gold potatoes
- 1 package of shirataki noodles
- ½ lb of beef, thinly sliced
- 8 pieces of snow peas
- 1 Tbsp of oil

For Seasonings

- 2 cups of dashi
- 4 Tbsp of mirin
- 4 Tbsp of soy sauce
- 2 Tbsp of sake
- 1 Tbsp of sugar

NUTRITION

Calories 338 Kcal | fat 11 g | Carbohydrate 39 g| Protein 17 g

INSTRUCTIONS

1. Slice the meat into quarters that are approximately 3 inches broad.
2. Slice onion into two and 1/2-inch-thick slices, then set aside.
3. Cut the carrots into 2.5 cm pieces once they have been peeled. Cutting carrot diagonal while turning it quarter between every cut is known as Rangiri in Japan. Cooking quicker and absorbing more flavors is made possible by increasing the amount of surface area.
4. Make four halves out of each potato. Smooth the corners of potatoes by removing the rough edges with a knife. Remove starch by soaking the potato in water for a few hours. Such a Japanese cutting method is referred to as a "mentor" in the industry. As a result, potatoes do not shatter. It is more probable that potatoes with sharp edges may collide with every other while cooking, causing them to break apart.
5. Remove the snow pea strings.
6. Put a pinch of salts into a small saucepan of boiling water. Incorporate snow peas.
7. Take these out of the water after one minute of cooking in the boiling water.
8. Cut shirataki noodles in two after draining them. Blanch noodles for one minute in the boiling water to get rid of the odor.
9. Do not throw away the water. Make three triangles out of thinly sliced meat.

10. Add onion to a big saucepan and sauté until translucent. Meat should be cooked till no pinker when the onion is covered with oil.

11. Please make sure the potatoes are well-coated with the cooking liquid before adding them. Make sure the potatoes don't break by applying a layer of this coating.

12. Make a sauce by mixing the carrots and shirataki noodles with soy sauce.

13. Add a little amount of dashi before stirring in the ingredients.

14. To cook, place a lid on the pan. Using a fine-mesh skimmer, remove foam and scum from the boiling liquid. Salt and pepper to taste.

15. A drop lid should be placed on the top of components after they've been mixed.

16. Simmer for 14 minutes on low heat or until a spear easily penetrates a potato. The Toshiba is essential for keeping the veggies in their proper form. As they become unsecured, they are more prone to breaking. While cooking, avoid mixing ingredients; otoshibuta will let flavour circulate on its own.

17. Remove otoshibuta by turning off the heat and lifting it out of the way. Let it out in the open for at least 30 to 60 minutes before serving as they cool; the tastes will infuse the components.

18. To Serve: you may reheat nikujaga by adding blanched snowy peas and covering the pot when you're ready to serve it. Allow the mixture to simmer for just a few mins before removing it from the heat. Make sure to add snow peas before serving to preserve their vibrant hue.

19. Nikujaga is ready to be served with some of the cooking liquid.

To Store : Refrigerate any leftovers for 4 days in an airtight jar or pot. The next day's Nikujaga is much better! Remove potatoes before freezing since they alter the texture. Up to a month may be stored in the freezer.

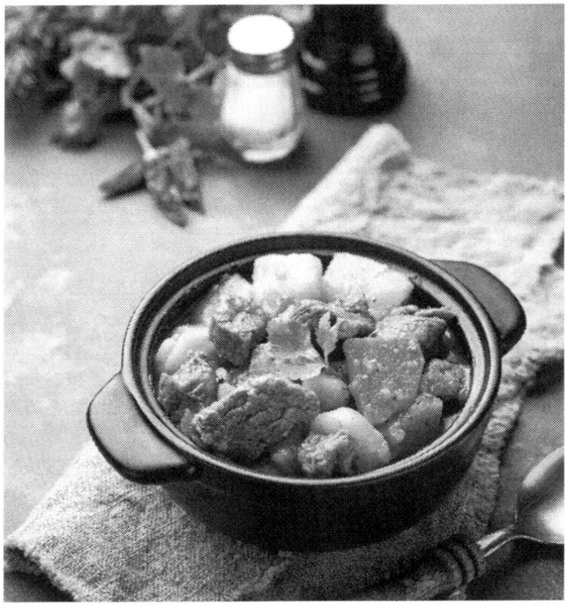

KINPIRA GOBO / BRAISED BURDOCK ROOT

Preparation — **15 MIN**

Cooking — **15 MIN**

Servings — **4**

INGREDIENTS

- 1 gobo
- 1/3 carrot
- 1 and ½ Tbsp of sesame oil, roasted

Seasonings:

- 1 Tbsp of sugar
- 1 Tbsp of sake
- 1 Tbsp of mirin
- 1 and ½ Tbsp of soy sauce
- For Garnish
- 2 tsp of sesame seeds, toasted

NUTRITION

Calories 139 Kcal | fat 6 g |
Carbohydrate 18 g|
Protein 2 g

INSTRUCTIONS

1. Gather all the necessary supplies. Preparing condiments before time is a promising idea, as well. All three ingredients may be mixed in a single dish.

THE ART OF PREPARATION

2. Avoid gobo with dark rings while searching for one. Unfortunately, local grocery shops don't always have the greatest gobo. Use a knife to shave away the dead skin. To avoid removing the gobo taste from under the skin, we don't use a vegetable peeler.
3. Shave the gobo and then cut it in half diagonally. Ideally, pieces should be no longer than 5 centimeters. Cutting the pieces into strips of thin julienne is next.
4. Gobo strips should be submerged in the water for 9 mins, with a water change occurring halfway through the time. Rinse them with icy water & dry them well after 9 mins.
5. Make thin 5 cm slices out of the carrots by peeling them and chopping them. Make thin julienne pieces by slicing them in half lengthwise.
6. Remove seeds from dried red chili pepper by cutting off the top and shaking the pepper. After that, thinly slice into rounds. Add seeds if you need them to be spicier. The seeds are frequently discarded in Japanese cuisine.

FOR COOKING

7. Warm sesame oil in a medium-sized frying pan. Add gobo after it's heated through.

8. Gobo should be sensitive after around two to three minutes. You'll need more minutes to stir fry gobo if you can't chop this into thin slices (thin slices cook quicker). Alternatively, you may add 34 cups of dashi and allow the gobo to boil for a few minutes before serving. Halfway through the cooking process, adding the carrot will ensure that the gobo is fully cooked.

9. Stir-fry the carrots and gobo for a few more minutes until soft.

10. Salt plus soy sauce are other good additions.

11. Add chili pepper once the seasonings have been well mixed into the veggies. It's done when there's no more liquid in it.

12. Add sesame seeds as well as stir everything together rapidly. The meal may be served separately or on a big plate or bowl.

Preserve: In an airtight container, you may keep leftovers in the refrigerator for three or four days/in the freezer for one month.

CARROT BEEF ROLLS

Preparation — **10 MIN**

Cooking — **30 MIN**

Servings — **2**

INGREDIENTS

- ¾ lb of beef, thinly sliced
- ¾ lb of carrots
- ¼ tsp of black pepper, freshly ground
- ¼ cup of potato starch
- 2 Tbsp of oil

For the Sauce

- 4 Tbsp of mirin
- 4 Tbsp of soy sauce

NUTRITION

Calories 307 Kcal | fat 17 g |
Carbohydrate 15 g|
Protein 19 g

INSTRUCTIONS

1. Gather all the necessary supplies.
2. Bring water to a boil in a medium-sized saucepan. If individuals do not have any access to finely sliced beef, you may follow these instructions to slice a block of the rib eye. Please keep in mind that each slice weighs around 20 grams.

TO MAKE THE BEEF AND CARROT ROLLS

3. Trim the ends of the carrot after it has been peeled.
4. Using a sharp knife, slice carrot in two lengthwise (or the thickness of your sliced meat).
5. Make thin julienned pieces out of the slabs.
6. In a pot of boiling water, cook julienned strips for 3 mins or till they are soft. Microwaving the carrot is an alternative method of cooking.
7. To get a general estimate of beef cuts, drain carrot strips & divide them accordingly.
8. Slice 2-3 pieces on a cutting board and place them on the cutting board. Spritz each piece of beef with black pepper before serving. Place carrot strips at one end of the beef slice and begin wrapping up.
9. Cook the remaining meat and carrots in the same manner.
10. Shake off any remaining potato starch before lightly coating the meat rolls.

TO MAKE THE BEEF AND CARROT ROLLS

11. Set a big frying pan to medium heat and prepare the ingredients. The oil should be uniformly distributed while the pan is heated. Put beef rolls in the heated oil. Work through batches rather than clogging up a skillet and risking overcooking the meat buns.

12. Transfer the beef rolls to a platter after they are evenly seared on both sides.

13. Set aside some time to finish the following batch. Add oil to the pan if required. Put beef rolls back into the pan after they've been seared to your liking.

14. You may quickly fry beef rolls and then add mirin with soy sauce to finish them off.

15. Toss beef rolls in the sauce as soon as it begins to sizzle. Remove from heat as the sauce will thicken fast due to potato starch in beef rolls.

16. Beef rolls may either be sliced in two or served whole. Enjoy!

To Store : Refrigerate any leftovers for up to 3 days or freeze them for up to a month in an airtight container.

SOBORO DON / CHICKEN BOWL

Preparation — **10 MIN**

Cooking — **20 MIN**

Servings — **2**

INGREDIENTS

For Ground Chicken

- 1 Tbsp of oil
- ½ lb pf ground chicken
- 1 tsp of ginger
- 1 Tbsp of sake
- 1 ½ Tbsp of sugar
- 1 Tbsp of mirin
- 2 Tbsp of soy sauce

For Scrambled Eggs

- 2 eggs large
- 1 Tbsp of sugar
- 1 Tbsp of oil

To Serve

- 2 serving short-grain rice cooked in Japanese
- ¼ cup of green peas
- red ginger pickled

NUTRITION

Calories 575 Kcal | fat 28 g | Carbohydrate 45 g| Protein 30 g

INSTRUCTIONS

1. Gather all the necessary supplies.

TO COOK GRAND CHICKEN

2. Using a frying pan, heat oil to moderate heat, then cook the chicken until it is pink in the middle. Cut meat into little parts using a wooden spoon.
3. Sugar plus mirin may be added as well.
4. As you add the soy sauce, continue to cut down the meat.
5. Keep ginger juice by grating it. Add ginger and juice to the meat once split up into small pieces.
6. Cook until all the liquid has evaporated. Set aside & clean the cooking pan as you do this.
7. To Cook Scrambled Eggs
8. Add sugar to the beaten eggs in a small bowl. Make sure the sugar is thoroughly dissolved by mixing well. Prep slew of long-handled kitchen utensils.
9. Pour the egg mixture into the frying pan that has been heated to a moderate flame.
10. Break the egg into little pieces with many chopsticks held in each hand. Transfer to a new bowl after it's finished cooking.

TO ASSEMBLE

11. You now have three different dishes of ingredients.

12. Put the steaming rice in the dishes and top with three ingredients as desired. Pickled ginger may be added to the dish as a finishing touch [kizami shoga], and enjoy!

To Store : You may keep leftovers for three to four days in the refrigerator and a month in the freezer in an airtight container.

SIMMERED BEEF & GINGER / SHIGURENI

Preparation — **5 MIN**

Cooking — **20 MIN**

Servings — **2**

INGREDIENTS

- ½ lb of beef, thinly sliced
- 1 ginger knob

Seasonings

- 2 Tbsp of sake
- 2 Tbsp of mirin
- 2 Tbsp of soy sauce
- 1 tsp of sugar

NUTRITION

Calories 319 Kcal | fat 16 g |
Carbohydrate 7 g|
Protein 25 g

To store : A few days in the fridge or a month in the freezer will keep it fresh.

INSTRUCTIONS

1. Make a list of everything you need,
2. Ginger should be peeled and sliced. Finally, julienne vegetables.
3. If you need to slice ribeye, follow this guide finely. Slice into 2-inch chunks.
4. 2 tablespoons sake, 2 tablespoons mirin, 2 tablespoons soy sauce, plus 1 teaspoon sugar go into a medium skillet. A simmer is achieved by adding julienned ginger.
5. Chopsticks may be used to divide the meat. Meat's fat will melt & form part of the sauce in about three minutes.
6. Simmer for 10 to 15 minutes at a low temperature or until the cooking fluid is completely absorbed.
7. Serve as soon as you see the bottom of the pot. Julienned ginger may be added to the dish as a garnish. Let cool fully before transferring to an airtight container.

TERIYAKI STEAK ROLLS

Preparation — 15 MIN

Cooking — 10 MIN

Servings — 2

INGREDIENTS

- 3 oz of carrot
- 3 oz of beans of French green
- ½ lb of beef, thinly sliced
- Sea salt or kosher
- black pepper, freshly ground
- 1 Tbsp of oil
- 2 Tbsp of sake

Teriyaki Sauce

- 3 Tbsp of soy sauce
- 2 Tbsp of sugar
- 2 Tbsp of sake
- 1 Tbsp of mirin

To store : A few days in the fridge or a month in the freezer will keep it fresh.

NUTRITION

Calories 319 Kcal | fat 16 g |
Carbohydrate 7 g|
Protein 25 g

INSTRUCTIONS

1. Make a list of everything you need. Ginger should be peeled and sliced. Finally, julienne vegetables. If you need to slice ribeye, follow this guide finely. Slice into 2-inch chunks.
2. 2 tablespoons sake, 2 tablespoons mirin, 2 tablespoons soy sauce, with 1 teaspoon sugar go into a medium skillet.
3. A simmer is achieved by adding julienned ginger. Chopsticks may be used to divide meat. Meat's fat may melt and form part of the sauce in about three mins.
4. Simmer for 10 to 15 minutes at a low temperature or until the cooking fluid is completely absorbed.
5. Serve as soon as you see the bottom of the pot. Julienned ginger may be added to the dish as a garnish. Allow cool fully before transferring to an airtight container.

YAKISOBA PAN / YAKISOBA DOG

Preparation — **15 MIN**

Cooking — **25 MIN**

Servings — **8**

INGREDIENTS

- 1 Tbsp of oil
- 8 buns hot dog
- 11 oz of yakisoba noodles
- 5 tbsp of Worcestershire sauce
- 1 tbsp of oyster sauce
- Aomori
- red ginger pickled
- Japanese mayonnaise (to serve)

INSTRUCTIONS

1. Gather all the necessary supplies.
2. Cut a small slit on the bread's surface (or side) to spread butter.
3. Make a half-dozen yakisoba noodles by cutting them in half.
4. Add 1 Tablespoon of oil to your frying pan and begin cooking the noodles.
5. Worcestershire sauce plus oyster sauce may be used to flavour noodles. Remove the pan from heat and combine the ingredients.
6. Make a yakisoba noodle sandwich with bread. Put aonori on top and a small piece of red ginger pickled in the middle. Wrap the sandwich in plastic wrap if you won't be eating it straight away.

NUTRITION

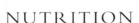

Calories 291 Kcal | fat 5 g |
Carbohydrate 51 g|
Protein 10 g

BEEF AND GREEN PEPPER STIR-FRY

Preparation — **15 MIN**

Cooking — **30 MIN**

Servings — **3**

INGREDIENTS

- ½ lb of beef, thinly sliced
- ½ shoot bamboo
- ½ bell pepper green
- 2 cloves garlic
- 1 ginger knob
- 2 Tbsp of oil

Marinade:

- 2 tsp of soy sauce
- 2 tsp of sake
- 1 tsp of oil, roasted sesame
- 1 tsp of potato starch
- black pepper, freshly ground
- Sauce: 1 ½ Tbsp of soy sauce
- 1 tsp of sugar
- 2 tsp of oyster sauce
- 1 Tbsp of sake
- 2 Tbsp of Chicken Stock
- 1 tsp of potato starch

NUTRITION

Calories 301 Kcal | fat 22 g |
Carbohydrate 8 g|
Protein 18 g

INSTRUCTIONS

1. Gather all the necessary supplies.

TO MAKE THE MARINADE AND SAUCE

2. Pour everything you need to make the marinade into a medium bowl, then whisk together until smooth. Season with salt plus black pepper to taste. Set aside for now.

3. Pour all the sauce ingredients into a small bowl, then whisk them until they form a smooth paste. Dispose of.

TO PREPARE THE BEEF

4. Thinly slice beef into cubes. Sukiyaki beef pre-cut into strips is used in this recipe. Shabu beef is thinner, whereas sukiyaki meat is thicker.

5. Incorporate the steak into the marinade by squeezing it with your hands. Dispose of.

FOR THE VEGETABLES

6. To make thin strips, slice pepper. If one's pepper is long, slice it in two lengthwise.

7. As with beef or bell pepper, thinly sliced bamboo shoots, cut bamboo stalk in two if too long. Cut them into equivalent strips using the best method. I begin by slicing the meat into thin slices.

8. It's difficult to cut bamboo into equal strips since it has a hollow center, but they do their best.

9. Crush (press) the garlic cloves plus mince ginger.

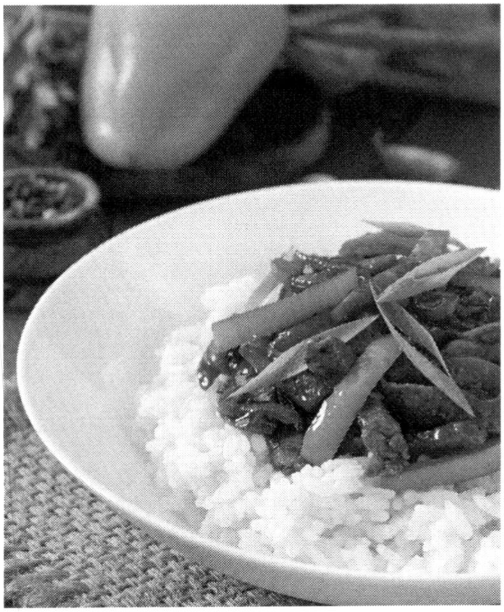

TO STIR FRY

10. Using moderate heat, pour 1 Tablespoon of oil into the wok, and coat the wok well using oil.

11. Stir-fry green pepper for about 5 mins, or till it is just soft. Bamboo shoots are pre-boiled before cooking to save time. Cook green pepper thoroughly before moving on.

12. Stir-fry bamboo shoots for a few mins or till they're soft and mushy. To serve, remove from heat & transfer to serving dish.

13. Put 1 Tablespoon of ginger, oil, and garlic into the pan and bring the heat back to medium. Cook till aromatic, stirring often.

14. Stir-fry meat till it is virtually no pinker in color.

15. Mix everything by putting stir-fried veggies back into the pan.

16. After whisking the sauce together, add it to meat and vegetables in a dish. The sauce might be thick as it cooks due to starch, so stir together everything one more time before serving.

17. Transfer to plate after being removed from the heat. Enjoy with a side of steaming rice!

To Store : Refrigerate any leftovers for 4 days in an airtight container.

OYAKODON / CHICKEN & EGG BOWL

Preparation — **15 MIN**

Cooking — **15 MIN**

Servings — **2**

INGREDIENTS

- chicken thighs are boneless, skinless
- ½ onion (85 g, 3 oz)
- 2 eggs large

For your Seasonings

- ½ cup of dashi (soup stock Japanese)
- 1 & ½ Tbsp of mirin
- 1 & ½ Tbsp of sake
- 1 & ½ Tbsp of soy sauce
- 1 & ½ tsp of sugar

For Serving

- 2 servings of short-grain rice Japanese cooked
- 2 sprigs of mitsuba (parsley Japanese) (or scallion/green onion)
- togarashi shichimi (seven spice Japanese)

NUTRITION

Calories 389 Kcal | fat 10 g | Carbohydrate 36 g| Protein 32 g

INSTRUCTIONS

FOR THE SEASONINGS MIXTURE

1. Gather all ingredients in a small bowl or measuring cup and mix them.
2. Stir in the sugar until it is completely dissolved. The amount of broth you use will vary according to the size of the pan. The leftovers will keep in the fridge for three days.

PREPARE THE INGREDIENTS

3. Onion and mitsuba, thinly sliced and chopped (or green onions). In a small dish, lightly beat one egg.
4. Chicken thighs should be sliced diagonally into approximately 1 &1/2-inches (4 cm) in length and 12-inches (1.3 cm) thick. Ensure that the chicken pieces are of the same thickness and maximize cooking surface area; the "sogigiri" cutting method is suggested.

TO COOK THE OYAKODON

5. Individual servings of Oyakodon are often prepared in this pan. While your egg is still a little runny, this pan makes it easy to transfer the final meal to the rice bowl. A tiny 8-inch (20cm) frying pan is used in this demonstration recipe. Halve all the ingredients before you begin. However, you may cook two portions in the same pan at once.
6. Remove the pan from the heat and arrange 1 dish of sliced onions in a thin layer in the pan. 1/3 to 1/2 of the spice's mixture should be poured in. Cover the onions with just enough sauce.

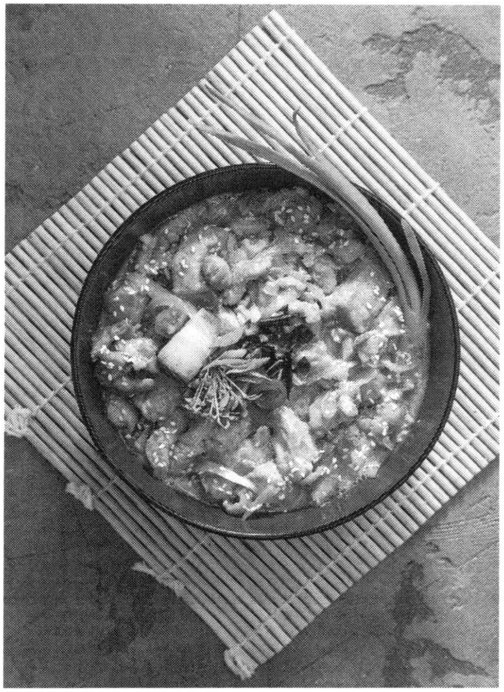

7. Toss in 1 serving of chicken and 1 serving of onions and serve immediately. It's important to divide the onion and chicken pieces equally. Bring it to your boil by increasing the temperature to medium.

8. Once the mixture reaches a boil, reduce the heat to medium-low. Remove any scum or foam that may have accumulated. Put a lid on the pan and heat for 5 minutes or unless the chicken isn't any longer pink & your onions are soft.

9. Try the broth & see whether you ought to alter it. Stir together the beaten egg and water in a small bowl. Pour over your chicken & onions. When the egg gets done as per your taste, cover the pan and cook on a moderate flame until it is. In Japan, the egg in oyakodon is served when it is nearly set but still runny.

10. Remove from the fire and add the mitsuba (green onion). On top of the steamed rice, place the egg, cooked chicken, and the rest of the sauce to your liking.

TO SERVE

11. Oyakodon may be served with a side of shichimi togarashi if desired.

To Store : It is possible to freeze any leftovers for up to one month or store them in the fridge for three days.

OMURICE / OMELETTE RICE

Preparation — **10 MIN**

Cooking — **20 MIN**

Servings — **2**

INGREDIENTS

- ¼ onion
- 4 mushrooms
- 4 slices of ham
- 1 Tbsp of neutral-flavored oil
- 3 Tbsp defrosted & drained green peas (if frozen)
- 1/8 tsp sea salt or kosher
- 1/8 tsp black pepper freshly ground
- 2 cups Japanese cooked short-grain rice
- 2 Tbsp divided unsalted butter

Tomato Sauce

- 3 tbsp of ketchup
- 4 Tbsp of paste tomato
- 2 Tbsp of water

Egg Mixture

- 4 eggs large
- 2 Tbsp divided milk

NUTRITION

> Calories 703 Kcal | fat 32 g |
> Carbohydrate 72 g|
> Protein 30 g

INSTRUCTIONS

TO MAKE THE SAUCE

1. Add the tomato paste, ketchup, and water to a small pot. Stir everything together until the sauce thickens. Set away for a later time.

TO PREPARE FRIED RICE

2. Slice the mushrooms after cleaning them with a moist cloth.
3. Slice the onion into little pieces and then cut it up.
4. Snip the meat into bite-sized pieces. Sauté onion in 1 tablespoon oil in a 10" frying pan.
5. Serve with ham, green peas, mushrooms, and other fixings.

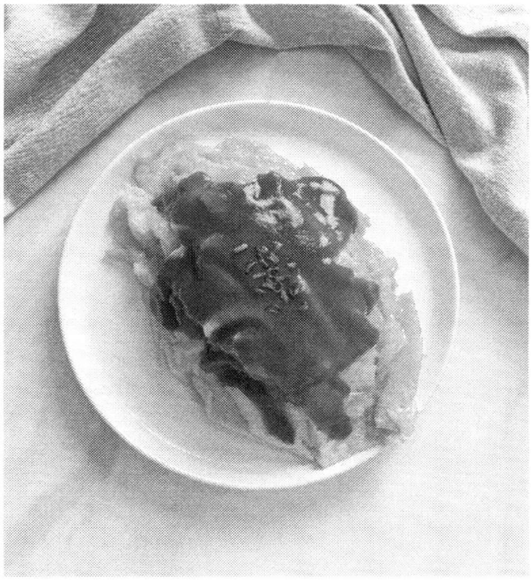

6. Sprinkle kosher salt & black pepper freshly ground is all you need for seasonings. Remove large bits of rice by chopping or slicing them into smaller pieces.

7. 3-4 tablespoons of tomato sauce may be added after the ingredients have been well mixed. Keep some sauce aside for drizzling on top of the finished dish. Take half your fried rice.

TO MAKE THE OMURICE (MAKES 2 OMURICE)

8. The first omurice should be tackled. Add eggs, milk, and a sprinkle of salt to a small bowl. Combine all of the ingredients in a bowl and whisk well.

9. Add butter to a new frying pan and bring it to medium-high heat. Add your beaten egg after the chocolate has melted.

10. Use chopsticks to whirl the food around the plate quickly. Add half of the ketchup rice to the center of the mixture after it has thickened but is still a little runny. Removing your pan from the fire and placing it over the moist cloth can help you burn yourself.

11. Wrap the rice in an egg omelet on both sides. There is no need to be faultless, but the "edge" surrounding your fried rice-containing omelette must be created.

12. When serving the omelet rice, place a serving dish beneath the pan, then turn the pan over.

13. Gently form the omelet into the football shape with a paper towel. To create the second omurice, follow the same steps as the first one.

14. Pour your tomato sauce on top of the Omurice before serving. You may either reheat your sauce or utilize room temp sauce for this recipe. The omurice should be garnished with parsley. Cheers!

To Store: You may store the leftovers in the fridge for up to three days or within the refrigerator for a month if they're sealed tightly.

GINGER PORK ROLLS W/ EGGPLANT

Preparation — **15 MIN**

Cooking — **15 MIN**

Servings — **2**

INGREDIENTS

- 2 eggplants Japanese
- ½ lb pork loin thinly sliced
- 2 Tbsp cornstarch or potato starch

For Seasonings:

- 1 ginger knob
- 2 Tbsp sauce soy
- 2 Tbsp of mirin
- 2 Tbsp water or the sake
- 1 tsp of sugar
- For Cooking:
- 1 Tbsp sesame oil roasted
- ½ tsp of miso

For Garnish:

- 4 leaves shiso (ooba / perilla)
- optional yuzu kosho (citrus chili Japanese paste)

NUTRITION

Calories 304 Kcal | fat 9 g | Carbohydrate 20 g| Protein 29 g

INSTRUCTIONS

1. All the sauce components should be mixed in a small bowl.
2. Use a peeler to remove the eggplant's skin and then soak the skin in water to remove any remaining sand or dirt.
3. Cut your eggplant into 2" (5 cm) wide strips, and then cut each strip into two halves.
4. Take off the bitterness & prevent the color from shifting by soaking each piece in the water for around 10 minutes.
5. Continue soaking the eggplant by slicing it into thin julienne strips.
6. A paper towel may remove any excess moisture from the eggplant.
7. Pork thinly cut is wrapped around two eggplant spears. Continue with the remaining pieces of pork until all the meat has been used.
8. Spread the meat with 1/2 of the corn/ potato starch sprinkled over the pork buns. On the other side, use the leftover potato or corn starch to create a slurry. Get rid of any extra starch.
9. Sesame oil should be heated on medium-high heat in a non-stick frying pan. Add pork rolls to the mix.Cook them to a golden-brown color on both sides.
10. Using a lid, cover the pan & cook on medium-low heat for about 2-3 minutes until your eggplant is fork-tender.

11. Take a pan and add the sauce. Coat your pork rolls by rotating & spooning some sauce over. Pour the sauce over the pork rolls and serve. Toss the eggplant peel and miso within the same pan without cleaning it beforehand.

12. In a medium saucepan, combine all ingredients and simmer for 2 to 3 minutes, occasionally stirring, until heated through. Top with the eggplant and serve. sing scissors, thinly slice the shiso leaves into long, narrow strips.

13. Shiso leaves provide a lovely garnish for the pork buns. Serve with a dash of yuzu kosho if you prefer it hot. You may sprinkle a little amount of it on top of the pork roll if you'd like.

SHOGAYAKI / GINGER PORK

Preparation — **10 MIN**

Cooking — **10 MIN**

Servings — **2**

INGREDIENTS

- 1 ginger knob
- ½ onion, chopped
- ¾ lb pork loin thinly sliced
- 1 Tbsp (for pork) sake
- 1 Tbsp plain flour all-purpose flour
- 1 to 2 Tbsp oil neutral-flavored (vegetable, canola, rice bran, etc.)
- black pepper freshly ground

Ginger Sauce

- 2 Tbsp sauce soy
- 2 Tbsp of mirin
- 3 Tbsp of sake
- 2 tsp of sugar

INSTRUCTIONS

TO MAKE THE GINGER SAUCE

1. Combine all ingredients for the ginger sauce in a mixing bowl.
2. Using a knife (or spoon), scrape off the ginger's outer peel and trim away any rough sections.
3. Keep the juice from the ginger when you use a grater. Grate the ginger & squeeze the juice out of it. 1 tablespoon of ginger juice is required.
4. It's OK to use up to 12 tbsp. of ginger juice (the remainder may be saved for another use). Adding 2-3 tsp. of ginger is what we do because we enjoy it.
5. Once the onion has been shredded to a consistency of 1 Tbsp grated onion plus juice, don't eat the remainder of the onion just yet.
6. Grate your onion, then add it to a ginger sauce.

TO PREPARE THE INGREDIENTS

7. The remainder of the onion should be thinly sliced.

8. This connective tissue (whitish region) between both the meat & fat should be sliced if the pork slice is longer than 1/8 inch (3 mm). When cooked, red meat & fat shrink & expand at varying rates, depending on their elasticity. When pan-frying pork slices, these incisions will keep them from curling up and keep them flat.

9. Pour the remaining ginger juice & 1 Tbsp of sake over the top.

10. If the pork strips are less than 1/8 inch (3mm) thick, you don't need to coat them in flour before cooking them. Lightly dust the pork pieces with flour before cooking. Retains pork moist and juicy by preventing it from drying out.

TO COOK THE PORK

11. Heat oil to a medium-high temperature in a big frying pan. Cook your pork slices inside a thin layer in a heated skillet, and then flip them over until the bottoms are golden brown on both sides. To ensure that the meat is seared and not overcooked, cook the meat in batches.

12. To prevent overcooking in the sauce, remove the pork from the pan when it is no longer pink in the middle and transfer it to a platter.

13. Adding oil (particularly if your skillet is non-stick) and onion after the pork is cooked is good.

14. Cook the onion for 6-8 minutes over medium heat, stirring occasionally. Add the meat back in when your onion is soft and transparent.

15. Pour your sauce over the meat once it has been mixed well. Simmer your sauce for around 2 minutes, then spoon it over the meat.

16. Transfer the sauce to a serving dish after it has reached the desired consistency.

To Store: You may store the leftovers in the fridge for up to three days or within the refrigerator for a month in an airtight container.

NUTRITION

Calories 361 Kcal | fat 13 g |
Carbohydrate 11 g|
Protein 40 g

ALL-PURPOSE MISO MEAT SAUCE

Preparation — **10 MIN**

Cooking — **20 MIN**

Servings — **4**

INGREDIENTS

- ¾ lb of ground pork
- 1 ginger knob
- ½ Tokyo of Negi
- 1 Tbsp of sesame oil, roasted
- 4 Tbsp of miso
- 2 Tbsp of sugar

Seasonings

- 3 Tbsp of mirin
- 3 Tbsp of sake
- 1 Tbsp of soy sauce
- 2 Tbsp of water
- 2 tsp of potato starch

NUTRITION

Calories 368 Kcal | fat 23 g | Carbohydrate 15 g| Protein 17 g

INSTRUCTIONS

1. In a bowl, grate the ginger and cut Negi into tiny pieces.
2. Mix 3 tablespoons mirin, 3 tablespoons sake, and 1 tablespoon soy sauce to produce seasonings.
3. In a small saucepan, combine the water with potato starch and bring to a boil. Add all ingredients and stir well until well combined in a large bowl.
4. A medium-sized frying pan should be heated to medium-high. Put 1 Tablespoon sesame oil with chopped Negi when the oil is heated. The Negi should be coated in oil till it is scented.
5. Break up the meat with your hands as you add it.
6. The beef should be cooked until it has lost its pink color, then add grated ginger & simmer for an additional minute or two.
7. Stir in miso plus sugar well.
8. Cook on low heat with the spices.
9. If you're satisfied with how much liquid is left, turn the heat down. If you need to consume meat sauce, you may leave sauce. Transfer to a dish or other container. Steamed rice or lettuce cups are good accompaniments.

To Store : There is a one-week shelf life for this product in the refrigerator. The only part that will be served should be reheated. Frozen for 3 to 4 weeks is another option.

MISO BUTTER SALMON

Preparation — **15 MIN**

Cooking — **15 MIN**

Servings — **2**

INGREDIENTS

- 2 salmon fillets
- sea salt or kosher
- black pepper freshly ground
- ½ Tbsp (plain flour) flour all-purpose
- mushrooms shimeji
- 1 Tbsp oil neutral-flavored (vegetable, canola, rice bran, etc.)
- mushrooms shiitake
- 1 tbsp butter unsalted

Seasonings

- 1 Tbsp of miso
- 2 Tbsp of sake
- 3 Tbsp of mirin
- 1 Tbsp sugar
- 1 & ½ Tbsp sauce soy
- Toppings
- chives
- sesame seeds toasted white

NUTRITION

Calories 397 Kcal | fat 20 g | Carbohydrate 11 g| Protein 36 g

INSTRUCTIONS

1. Make a list of everything you need.
2. In a bowl, mix the seasoning ingredients: 1 Tbsp of sugar, 1 Tbsp of mirin, 2 Tbsp of sake, and 1 Tbsp of soy sauce.
3. Chives and shimeji mushrooms should be finely chopped. With your hands, break up the shimeji into tiny pieces.
4. Remove the stems from the shiitake mushrooms & slice them very thinly before serving.
5. Take a pair of tweezers to remove any bone from your salmon if it does have some. Season your salmon using kosher salt & black pepper freshly ground after patting it dry using a paper towel.
6. Thinly cover the fish with flour before sprinkling it on. By adding flour, you'll be able to keep the delectable salmon juices within the fish and thicken the sauce.
7. In a medium-sized frying pan, warm the olive oil. When preparing the salmon, place it on its flesh side. The edge of a fillet shows how far you've cooked. Avoid overcooking your fish to a crisp. For around 5 minutes, cook.
8. Add your shimeji & shiitake mushrooms after

flipping the pan over so the peel side is over the bottom of the pan. For around 5 minutes, cook the skin side.

9. After that, cook the salmon's sides for one minute. Even if there's a little transparent pink in the center, don't worry about it. The fish should keep cooking as the residual heat dissipates.

10. Sauté your mushrooms in butter until they are tender. To get as much sauce as possible onto your fish, put mushrooms on it before cooking! Using a spoon, coat the salmon with the spices. Add chives as a garnish to the fish.

SOY-VINEGAR PICKLED CUCUMBERS

Preparation — **10 MIN**

Cook Time — **5 MIN**

Servings — **12**

INGREDIENTS

- ¼ cup of water
- ¼ cup of soy sauce
- ¼ cup of sushi vinegar
- ¼ cup of sugar
- 2 English cucumbers large

INSTRUCTIONS

1. In a medium saucepan, combine water, vinegar, soy sauce, & sugar, then bring to a boil over moderate flame. Take a break and let the mixture cool down before serving.
2. Cucumbers should be chopped into medium-sized pieces.
3. Place the cucumbers in a big glass jar or another container with a tight-fitting cover for storage.
4. Cover the container & pour the soy-vinegar mix over the cucumbers. Freeze for at least eight hours and up to a day while the cucumbers marinade. The best way to get an even coating of seasoning on the cucumbers while they're marinating is to regularly turn them.

NUTRITION

Calories 60 Kcal | fat 5 g |
Carbohydrate 30 g |
Protein 8 g

TERIYAKI SALMON

Preparation — **10 MIN**

Cooking — **10 MIN**

Servings — **2**

INGREDIENTS

- 2 salmon fillets skin-on
- ¼ tsp sea salt or kosher
- 1/8 tsp black pepper freshly ground
- 1 Tbsp (plain flour) flour all-purpose
- ½ Tbsp neutral-flavored oil (vegetable, canola, rice bran)
- 1 tbsp butter unsalted
- 1 Tbsp wine Chinese rice or sake
- For the Teriyaki Sauce
- 1 Tbsp wine Chinese rice or sake
- 1 Tbsp of mirin (substitute the 1 Tbsp's water/sake plus 1 tsp of sugar)
- 1 Tbsp of sugar
- 2 Tbsp sauce soy

NUTRITION

Calories 274 Kcal | fat 13 g | Carbohydrate 9 g| Protein 24 g

INSTRUCTIONS

1. The teriyaki sauce may combine the sauce components and stir well unless the sugar has dissolved. Rinse the fish and wipe it dry before cooking it. Both sides of the salmon should be seasoned with kosher salt & black pepper.
2. One side of a salmon should be uniformly coated with 1/2 Tbsp of all-purpose flour. Sprinkle the remaining flour on the opposite side of the dough. Remove any extra flour with a spatula.
3. Over medium-high heat, place a frying pan. Add the oil and butter to the mixture. Butter may burn if you're not careful. Reduce your heat or take the frying pan from it if it becomes too hot.
4. The salmon fillets should be placed skin-side down in the pan. Flip the salmon after 3 minutes of cooking when the base becomes golden brown.
5. Cover the pan with a lid after adding the sake. Salmon should be steamed for around 3 minutes unless it reaches an internal temperature of 140 degrees Fahrenheit. Transfer your salmon to the serving dish.
6. When you've added the teriyaki flavor, you'll want to raise the pan's temperature. Pour some of the sauce on the salmon as soon as it simmers.
7. Turn off the heat after the sauce has thickened. Serve your salmon on a serving platter as soon as possible.

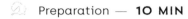

8. Pour your sauce over the meat once it has been mixed well. Simmer your sauce for around 2 minutes, then spoon it over the meat.
9. Transfer the sauce to a serving dish after it has reached the desired consistency.

To Store : You may keep the remainder for up to three days in the fridge and two weeks in the freezer in a sealed jar.Cook the onion for 6-8 minutes over medium heat, stirring occasionally. Add the meat back in when your onion is soft and transparent.

SHRIMP FRIED RICE

Preparation — **10 MIN**

Cooking — **10 MIN**

Servings — **2**

INGREDIENTS

- 4 oz shelled & deveined shrimps (6 shrimp;)
- 1 lettuce leaf iceberg
- 1 green scallion/onion
- 2 Tbsp oil neutral-flavored (vegetable, canola, rice bran)
- 1 egg large
- 1 Tbsp sesame oil roasted
- 1 tsp of sake
- 1/8 to ¼ tsp sea salt or kosher
- 2 cups Japanese rice short grain cooked
- 1/8 tsp powder white pepper
- black pepper freshly ground
- 1 tsp sauce soy

NUTRITION

Calories 526 Kcal | fat 25 g |
Carbohydrate 55 g|
Protein 20 g

INSTRUCTIONS

1. Check out our guide on washing shrimp if yours haven't been deveined and shelled already. Shrimp should be cut into 1/2-inch (1.3 cm) cubes.
2. Lettuce and onion should be chopped into tiny bits.
3. In a small bowl, gently whisk the egg.
4. Add the oil to the wok and stir it around until it covers the whole surface. Immediately after putting in the egg, bring the temperature up to high. As soon as you add enough oil to the pan, your egg will not adhere to it. When its 80 percent done, please remove it from the pan and serve it on a platter.
5. Add shrimp to the wok, followed by sake and salt. Cook the shrimp until they become a darker shade of pink on the exterior. There's no need to overcook the insides at this point. Shrimp should be served on a platter.
6. Stir in sesame oil and sauté the scallion until it's well coated in the oil, then remove from the heat.
7. Take a fork and mash the bits of rice together. Toss everything together in a wok.
8. Return the egg & shrimp to the pan and stir with the rice after being covered with oil. Salad greens, white pepper, black freshly ground pepper, & soy sauce should all be included. Toss and stir the contents of the pan often. Serve right away.

NIRATAMA DONBURI / CHIVE & EGG RICE BOWL

Preparation — **5 MIN**

Cooking — **5 MIN**

Servings — **2**

INGREDIENTS

- 3 eggs large
- 1 tsp of sake
- ½ tsp sauce soy
- ¼ tsp sea salt kosher
- black pepper freshly ground
- 2 Tbsp oil neutral-flavored (vegetable, canola, rice bran, etc.)
- 1 & ½ oz garlic chives (Nira or Chinese chives) (pat dry & rinsed)
- 2 servings of cooked short-grain rice Japanese

INSTRUCTIONS

1. In a mixing bowl, combine your eggs, sake, salt, soy sauce, & black pepper (but don't over mix).
2. To prepare fresh garlic chives, trim them to a length of 2" (5 cm).
3. In a wok or frying pan, heat 12 tbsp oil and sauté the bottom white portion of the garlic chives until softened, about 1 minute. After that, swiftly stir-fry the green portion. Add oil & cook the meat/seafood first, then move to a serving dish. Afterward, return to the pan/wok with the egg mixture.
4. Add the garlic chives to the egg mixture in the bowl.
5. Add the remaining oil to the pan and bring it to a boil. Add your egg & garlic chive mix to the pan after the wok is heated and the smoke is poured. The egg mix will become light and airy as it cools. Gently fold the egg mixture from the middle outwards.
6. The egg & garlic chives should be served over the rice when your egg is nearly done cooking.
7. You may keep the leftovers in the fridge for up to three days and two weeks in the refrigerator in a sealed jar.

NUTRITION

Calories 323 Kcal | fat 17 g |
Carbohydrate 28 g|
Protein 12 g

KIMCHI FRIED RICE

Preparation — **5 MIN**

Cooking — **15 MIN**

Servings — **2**

INGREDIENTS

- 2 green scallions/onions
- 2 garlic cloves
- 1 cup cabbage kimchi napa
- 2 Tbsp drained kimchi juice
- 2 Tbsp oil neutral-flavored (vegetable, canola, rice bran)
- 2 tsp of gochujang (chili paste Korean)
- ½ Tbsp sauce soy
- 2 servings of short-grain rice Japanese cooked
- 1 tsp sesame oil roasted
- 1 tsp sesame seeds toasted white
- black pepper freshly ground
- For Serving
- 5 seaweed Korean (shredded, optional)
- 2 eggs large

NUTRITION

Calories 351 Kcal | fat 21 g | Carbohydrate 31 g| Protein 9 g

INSTRUCTIONS

1. Make a list of everything you need. In this case, it's best to let the rice sit at room temperature for a few minutes on a baking sheet coated with parchment paper until the moisture evaporates. Add 14 kg of protein and vegetables to build your variation (cut into bite-size). Pork is one of my favorite meats. Before adding the scallion, cook the meat.
2. Use a mandoline to slice the white portion of the onion into thin slices, and then chop the green pieces in half. Garlic cloves should also be minced.
3. Cut the kimchi into bite-sized pieces with kitchen shears.
4. Garlic and scallion (white portion) minced in oil in a big wok over high heat. While stirring continuously, bring to a boil.
5. Cook the kimchi & kimchi juice for one minute with the scallion before adding them.
6. Stir in the gochujang & soy sauce, then simmer for around 1 minute more, or until the kimchi softens before serving. Add water or kimchi juice if the kimchi begins to cling to the base but isn't cooked through. If you want your food spicier, you may add extra kimchi juice before adding rice; cook kimchi fully.
7. Stir in the rice, then turn the heat down to a simmer. The rice should be warmed through in about a minute or two. To prevent the contents from adhering to the base of the wok, toss the wok often during cooking.

8. In the last step, drizzle sesame seeds, sesame oil, and the green portion of the scallion on top. Black pepper should be added towards the end. Toss the wok around a few times a day to keep everything fresh. Ensure that the ingredients aren't burning and sticking together before removing them from the pan.

9. The eggs should be cooked in a non-stick frying pan over medium heat while the oil is heated. Add salt and pepper and simmer until the egg whites are set but still runny. Using a spoon, scoop some hot oil from the pan & pour it over an unprepared egg white to ensure that the egg white cooks quicker without overcooking the yolk.

10. Scallions & Korean seaweed are sprinkled on the Kimchi Fried Rice before adding a fried egg.

To Store : You may keep the leftovers for up to two days in the fridge and a month in the refrigerator in an airtight container.

STIR-FRIED VEGETABLES / YASAI ITAME

Preparation — **55 MIN**

Cooking — **10 MIN**

Servings — **4**

INGREDIENTS

- 6.5 oz pork thinly sliced
- 10 peas snow
- ¼ onion
- ½ carrot
- 1 garlic clove
- ¼ cabbage
- 1 ginger knob
- 1 Tbsp oil neutral-flavored (vegetable, canola, rice bran)
- 3.5 oz sprouts bean (loosely packed 2 cups)
- For Pork Marinade
- 1 tsp of sake
- 1 tsp sauce soy

Seasonings

- 2 tsp sauce oyster
- 1 tsp sauce soy
- ½ tsp of sea salt or kosher
- black pepper freshly ground
- 2 tsp sesame oil roasted

NUTRITION

Calories 158 Kcal | fat 8 g | Carbohydrate 10 g | Protein 13 g

INSTRUCTIONS

1. Make a list of everything you need.
2. Smaller chunks of beef may be cut and marinated in a small dish with 1 tbsp of soy sauce & 1 tsp of sake.
3. Take off the snow pea threads and slice the onion.
4. Cut your cabbage into 1" (2.5 cm) cubes and set aside.
5. First, chop the carrot into 2" (5 cm)-long slabs to make matchsticks.
6. The garlic and ginger should be minced.
7. Add 1 Tbsp of vegetable oil to a large wok or frying pan and bring to medium-high heat. Add your ginger and garlic when the oil is heated.
8. When the spices are aromatic, add your meat & simmer until it is approximately 80 % done. Alternatively, you may cook until the meat is no longer pink, remove it, and then return it

to the pot when the vegetables are roasted to your liking. It will ensure that the meat doesn't become over-done.

9. Onion is added and stir-fried until it's almost tender. After that, add the carrots. You should start with the rougher and thicker veggies first to add other vegetables that aren't included in the recipe.

10. Toss in the snow peas and cabbage as soon as the carrots have softened up. The components should be continually tossed and stirred.

11. Then, add your bean sprouts & stir once more before removing them from heat. A dash of oyster sauce and a dash of soy sauce goes a long way.

12. A couple of tbsp of sesame oil, black pepper & salt complete the dish. Take a bite right away and pair it with rice & miso soup for a delicious dinner experience.

13. The leftovers may be stored in a sealed jar within the refrigerator for three days or in the freezer for two weeks.

WAFU HAMBAGU

Preparation — **20 MIN**

Cooking — **30 MIN**

Servings — **4**

INGREDIENTS

- ½ onion, sliced
- 1 & ½ Tbsp oil neutral-flavored (vegetable, canola, rice bran)
- ¼ cup Japanese breadcrumbs/panko
- 2 Tbsp of milk
- ½ lb beef ground
- ½ lb pork ground
- 1 egg large
- 1 garlic clove (minced or crushed)
- ¼ tsp of nutmeg
- 2 tsp sea salt or kosher
- black pepper freshly ground

For Cooking Patties

- 1 & ½ Tbsp oil neutral-flavored (vegetable, canola, rice bran)
- Toppings
- 3-inch radish daikon
- 2 leaves shiso (perilla / ooba) (for garnish scallion / green onion)
- Sauce
- ½ ponzu cup
- 1 sugar tsp
- ¼ tsp kosho yuzu

INSTRUCTIONS

1. Onion minced finely. Sauté your onion in 1 1/2 Tbsp of oil in the frying pan until golden brown. Toss the mixture into a big bowl and allow it to cool completely.
2. Combine the panko & the milk in a bowl. Combine everything in a big bowl after the onion has cooled.
3. Combine all ingredients and knead until dough is sticky about 5 minutes.
4. Four pieces of the mixture should be made. A little oil on your hands will keep the meat from sticking to your fingers.
5. Ten times toss each part between your palms to expel the air from the mixture.
6. Patties should be oval-shaped. The top should be more circular than flat, as it is with most hamburger patties. Plastic wrap and a 30-minute chill in the fridge are the best ways of ensuring well-combined patties before cooking

NUTRITION

Calories 367 Kcal | fat 27 g |
Carbohydrate 6 g|
Protein 23 g

7. Peel the daikon and grind it into a fine paste. Daikon should be squeezed dry. Remove the shiso's stem and roll it into a ball. Cut into thin ribbons or juliennes. Slice the onion thinly if you're substituting it.

8. To prepare the sauce, whisk together all the yuzu kosho, ponzu, & sugar till the sugar is completely dissolved.

9. When 1 12 Tbsp oil is hot, carefully lay the patties in the pan. Because the middle of every patty would rise & expand when heated, indent it with your fingertips. Do not rotate the patties until they have browned for around 3 to 4 minutes. Cook your patties for 4 to 5 minutes on the other side, covered, over medium heat until the meat is well cooked.

10. Raise the temperature to medium-high before adding sauce to a pan. Cook the meat for approximately 2 minutes while spooning the sauce over it with a spoon.Serve the patties on a serving tray. While scraping off fat from the sauce, lower the heat slightly. Place the sauce inside a small serving dish and serve.

11. Garnish the beef patties with grated daikon and shiso before serving (or scallion). Add the excess sauce over the top when you're ready to eat.

OSHITASHI / SPINACH & SESAME SEEDS V

Preparation — **5 MIN**

Cooking — **3 MIN**

Servings — **2**

INGREDIENTS

- 1 bag spinach pre-washed
- 1 tsp oil sesame
- 1 tsp seeds sesame
- 1 tsp sauce soy
- ½ tsp mirin

NUTRITION

Calories 64 Kcal | fat 4 g | Carbohydrate 6 g | Protein 4.5 g

INSTRUCTIONS

1. Boil a saucepan of water with a little amount of salt in it. Cook the spinach for one minute in boiling water. Do not wait until it is wilted to remove the spinach from the dish. Shock this in a dish of iced water & icy water for a few moments.

2. To remove as much water as possible from the spinach, remove it from the icy water and gently compress it. The final product should be around the size of a golf ball. Remove the stems and carefully separate the leaves by chopping them into smaller pieces.

3. Soy sauce, sesame seeds, mirin, & sesame oil go into a dish with spinach. Serve immediately after mixing well.

JAPANESE COLESLAW SALAD

Preparation — **5 MIN**

Cooking — **0 MIN**

Servings — **4**

INGREDIENTS

- 3 cups coleslaw mix (pre-shredded)

For dressing:

- 1 tsp sugar granulated
- 2 tsp soy sauce light
- 1 tsp oil canola
- 2 & ½ tbsp vinegar rice wine
- 1 finely chopped stalk scallion

Toppings:

- 3 tbsp sesame seeds toasted
- ¼ cup flakes bonito

INSTRUCTIONS

1. Grab a wooden bowl and add all the ingredients for the dressing. Mix well.
2. Pour the dressing over the shredded coleslaw mixture.
3. Sprinkle sesame seeds & bonito flakes on top of the dish before serving.

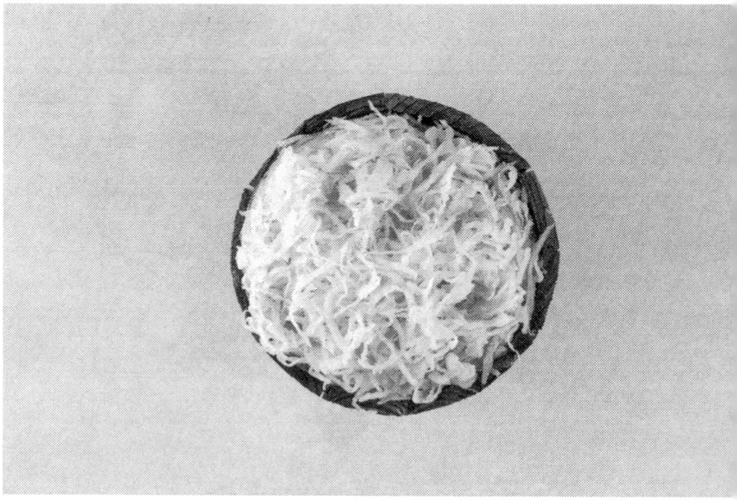

NUTRITION

Calories 149 Kcal | fat 9 g |
Carbohydrate 14 g |
Protein 5 g

ONIGIRI / JAPANESE RICE BALLS

Preparation — **5 MIN**

Cooking — **15 MIN**

Servings — **4**

INGREDIENTS

- 3 cups of cooked grain rice Japanese short
- salt kosher

Okaka

- Salted Salmon
- Mushroom plus Scallion
- Rice Seasoning Japanese
- Okaka
- ½ cup bonito flakes dried
- 1 tbsp sauce soy

Salted Salmon

- 1 small salmon piece
- salt kosher
- Mushrooms & Scallions
- ¼ cup straw mushrooms canned
- ½ tbsp sauce soy
- 1 tbsp mirin
- ¼ tsp sugar granulated
- 1 minced scallion
- Furikake
- the seasoning packet of Japanese rice

INSTRUCTIONS

OKAKA

1. Add dry bonito flakes & soy sauce to a medium bowl and mix well. Stir until the bonito flakes have absorbed all the soy sauce. Set away for later.

SALTED SALMON

2. Set the temperature of the oven to 400 degrees Fahrenheit.
3. Transfer the salmon fillet to a parchment-lined baking sheet & sprinkle all sides using salt.

NUTRITION

Calories 94 Kcal | fat 0.2 g | Carbohydrate 20 g | Protein 2 g

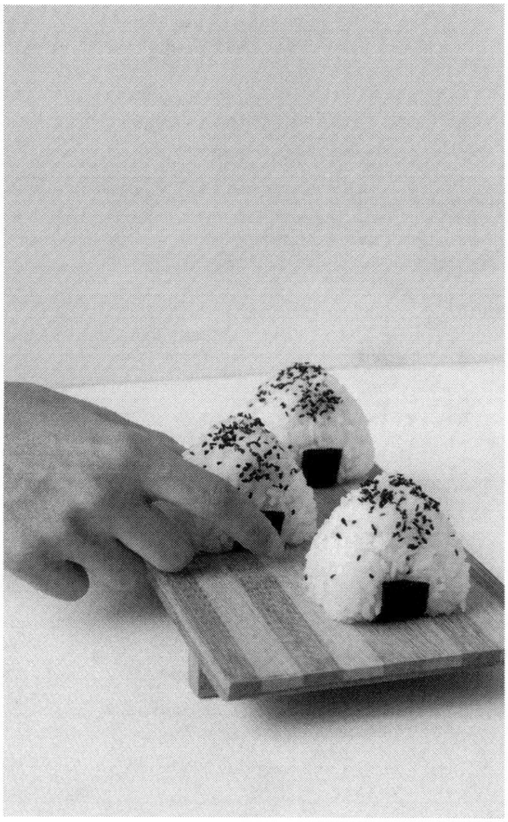

4. It takes around 25 minutes to roast at 400 degrees F.

5. Set the cooked fish aside & flake it using chopsticks or a fork.

MUSHROOMS AND SCALLIONS

6. Add the mushrooms, soy sauce, mirin, and sugar to a small saucepan and warm over medium heat. Cook the mushrooms until they have soaked the liquid.

7. Transfer the mixture to a bowl & turn off the heat. Shallots are added after the mixture has been allowed to reach room temperature.

HOW TO SHAPE ONIGIRI

8. Cut a nori sheet in half and then in half again to make three pieces. Set away for later.

9. Set up a small bowl of water within your work area. Prepare your ingredients here. Take a sip of water. As a result, the rice won't adhere to your hands as much.

10. In the palms of your damp hand, take a third to half of a cup of rice.

11. You may do this by pushing your thumb into the middle of the rice.

12. Add half a spoonful of filling towards the depression in the middle and gently press it in place.

13. Gently press your rice between the hands to form rounds or triangles. Keep the pressure light.

14. Onigiri's exterior is spiced up with a sprinkle of kosher salt.

15. Wrap the onigiri with a piece of nori, much as you would a blanket.

16. Use a little filler to mark which flavor while preparing a few onigiri.

17. Repeat these processes with the remaining rice and place it on a platter. Serve.

FURIKAKE ONIGIRI

18. Furikake spice, if desired, should be sprinkled over the boiled rice and thoroughly mixed in. Serve rice that has been formed into triangles or balls.

NASU DENGAKU

Preparation — **5 MIN**

Cooking — **10 MIN**

Servings — **2**

INGREDIENTS

- 2 small eggplants
- 2 tbsp oil vegetable
- ¼ cup miso paste
- 2 tbsp mirin
- 1 tbsp sugar granulated
- 1 tbsp sake
- seeds sesame

INSTRUCTIONS

1. The interior of the eggplant should be scored into tiny squares with a knife after it has been cut in half.
2. Place the eggplant skin-side down in a hot pan with oil.
3. To brown the skin, cook for another few minutes at a medium heat level. Cover the eggplant with a lid and cook for another 30 minutes. Ensure that the eggplant has been cooked through before moving on.
4. Dissolve mirin and sugar in sake, and then add miso to taste.
5. Place your eggplant on a baking sheet covered in foil and bake. Brush every eggplant with miso dengaku mix until it is completely covered.
6. Broil for around 4 minutes in the oven. When you remove the miso mixture from the oven, it should be bubbling.
7. Serve immediately with the sesame seeds sprinkled on top.

NUTRITION

Calories 288 Kcal | fat 16 g | Carbohydrate 28 g | Protein 5 g

JAPANESE CURRY RECIPE

Preparation — **15 MIN**

Cooking — **60 MIN**

Servings — **4**

INGREDIENTS

- 2 tbsp oil peanut
- 1 lb chopped stewing beef
- 1 large peeled & finely chopped onion
- 2 cloves minced garlic
- 1 tbsp peeled & minced ginger
- 1 peeled, grated, finely chopped apple
- 3 tbsp flour all-purpose
- 2 carrots large
- 1 potato large
- 1 tsp masala garam
- 4 tbsp powder curry
- 2 tbsp paste tomato
- 2 cups of red wine
- 2 tbsp sugar granulated
- 2 tbsp sauce soy
- 4 cups of water

NUTRITION

Calories 506 Kcal | fat 31 g |
Carbohydrate 33 g |
Protein 21 g

INSTRUCTIONS

1. Add peanut oil to a large saucepan over medium-high heat, and then add the stewing meat. Cook for 5 minutes, or until the meat is well done. Place on a platter and put away.
2. Reduce the heat to medium-low and sauté the onions in the remaining 1 tbsp of peanut oil for 10 minutes, or until transparent and slightly caramelized.
3. 2 minutes after putting in the garlic, ginger, & apple, simmer for another minute. One minute later, add the flour and mix.
4. Then add the carrots and potatoes, the garam masala & curry powder, and mix everything well.
5. Add tomato paste, mix well, gently add wine, then bring to a boil.
6. Stir in the remaining sugar, soy sauce, and water before bringing it to a boil. As soon as you put in the steak, decrease the heat to a gentle simmer. For 30 min, cover & cook.
7. Remove the cover and simmer the curry soup for a further 30 minutes, or until it has reduced by about a third. Serve the rice with the seasonings.

OKONOMIYAKI / OSAKA PANCAKES

Preparation — **30 MIN**

Cooking — **30 MIN**

Servings — **4**

INGREDIENTS

For the Okonomiyaki:

- 2 cups flour all-purpose
- 1 & ¼ cup soup stock dashi
- 1-2 lb cabbage, chopped
- 4-6 tbsp chopped divided green onion
- 1 cup tenkasu, or divided tempura flakes
- 4-6 divided large eggs
- 1 tsp vegetable oil
- 12-18 thin strips of pork

For the Toppings:

- 1 dash sauce okonomiyaki
- Mayonnaise
- 1 aonori pinch
- Handful katsuobushi or bonito flakes dried
- Beni-shoga or red ginger pickled

NUTRITION

Calories 534 Kcal | fat 21 g | Carbohydrate 47 g | Protein 38 g

INSTRUCTIONS

MAKE THE OKONOMIYAKI

1. In a medium bowl, combine the flour and baking powder.
2. Add dashi to the bowl and whisk to create a batter. Then chill for an hour or so before serving.
3. You'll need around half a cup of batter for each okonimiyaki pancake.
4. Chopped green onion, cabbage, & tempura flake batter are all that is needed to make this dish.
5. Add one egg to the batter and mix it well.
6. Preheat your electric skillet or griddle and drizzle in a little oil when ready to cook.
7. Make a circle with the batter in the pan. Constantly check on it; this would take a couple of minutes to cook.
8. Meanwhile, in a separate skillet, brown a few slices of meat & top the okonomiyaki with it.
9. During the cooking process, flip the okonomiyaki.
10. As indicated in the recipe, top the okonomiyaki with the garnishes. Continue this process unless the batter has been consumed.
11. Garnish With Toppings. Spread your okonomiyaki sauce & mayonnaise over top of the okonomiyaki before flipping it over one more.
12. Add ao-nori to the sauce and mix it in. If desired, top with katsuobushi & beni-shoga.

ROYAL OKONOMIYAKI

Preparation — **10 MIN**

Cooking — **10 MIN**

Servings — **3**

INGREDIENTS

- 1 cup okonomiyaki flour Osaka style
- ¾ cup of dashi
- 10 oz green cabbage
- 2 scallions
- 2 eggs
- 2 tbsp oil neutral
- 1 cup of beans sprouts

Toppings

- flakes Bonito
- red ginger Pickled
- regular mayonnaise or Kewpie mayonnaise
- tonkatsu sauce or Okonomi sauce
- green laver Aonori

NUTRITION

Calories 291 Kcal | fat 9 g |
Carbohydrate 42 g |
Protein 12 g

INSTRUCTIONS

1. A big bowl should mix the flour & dashi broth.
2. Toss the batter with the cabbage, scallions, & eggs until everything is well-combined.
3. 1 tbsp. Oil, heated to medium-high, in a large skillet. Swirl to cover the pan.
4. Shape the remaining batter into a ½-inch-thick pancake by spooning a third of it into the pan. Make sure the bottom becomes golden brown before adding another 1/3 cup of bean sprouts & cook for another 4 minutes.
5. Flip your pancake and heat for 3 minutes to cook the bean sprouts.
6. Top with pickled ginger, okonomi sauce, bonito flakes, kewpie mayonnaise, and aonori on a serving platter.
7. To make the remaining two pancakes, use the same procedure.

JAPANESE FRIED RICE

Preparation — **10 MIN**

Cook Time — **5 MIN**

Servings — **4**

INGREDIENTS

- 1 tbsp oil vegetable
- 2 cloves minced garlic
- 1 finely chopped onion or small leek
- 1 small finely chopped carrot
- 300 Japanese rice grams
- 1 cup shredded lettuce
- 2 whisked large eggs
- 1 tbsp sauce soy
- salt & white pepper ground

INSTRUCTIONS

1. Add the oil and garlic to a wok or big skillet on high heat and sauté for 30 seconds.
2. Cook the onions and carrots for 1 to 2 mins, or until they are tender but still have their crisp. Add the other ingredients.
3. Stir in the rice & lettuce once it's been cooked till the ingredients are quite well.
4. Add eggs to one side of the rice. Eggs should be constantly stirred and broken until they are almost done.
5. Soy sauce & eggs with fried rice are a delicious combination.
6. Make sure to properly distribute your ingredients throughout the fried rice by sprinkling them with salt & pepper and stirring. Allow cooling before serving.

NUTRITION

Calories 183 Kcal | fat 5 g | Carbohydrate 29 g | Protein 6 g

HAYASHI GROUND BEEF CURRY

Preparation — **10 MIN**

Cook Time — **16 MIN**

Servings — **2**

INGREDIENTS

- 1/3 peeled & diced carrot
- 1 onion medium
- 1 tbsp oil canola
- 150 g ground beef lean
- 1 tsp starch corn
- 1 cup of broth beef
- 2 tbsp ketchup
- 1 tbsp sake
- 1 tbsp sauce Worcestershire
- 1 egg boiled

INSTRUCTIONS

1. Cut the onion in half. You'll need to use half of it for frying and the rest for the dry curry. This may be done by cutting one half into quarters. Chop the second one up into little pieces.
2. Boil the egg and then chop or mash it with a fork into tiny pieces. Use salt and pepper to taste. Add onions & carrots to the hot oil. For around 3 minutes, cook.
3. Add corn starch to the veggies and ground meat before serving. Stir in ¼ cup of beef broth while breaking up the ground meat. When the meat is no longer pink, remove it and set it aside from the pan.
4. Bring to a boil and then reduce the heat to low. When the liquid has evaporated, cook for another 10 minutes or so. Use salt & pepper to taste.
5. In a separate pan, cook the onions until they are crispy. Curry, eggs, & fried onions go on top of rice in a serving bowl.

NUTRITION

Calories 525 Kcal | fat 12 g |
Carbohydrate 71 g |
Protein 27 g

JAPANESE DASHI ROLLED OMELET

Preparation — **5 MIN**

Cook Time — **3 MIN**

Servings — **1**

INGREDIENTS

- 2 eggs large
- 3 tbsp dashi broth
- 1 tsp soy sauce
- ¼ cup of finely chopped scallions
- 1 tbsp vegetable oil
- grated daikon
- soy sauce
- bonito flakes

INSTRUCTIONS

1. Combine the eggs, soy sauce, and dashi in a mixing dish to make the egg mixture.
2. Stir in scallions.
3. Use a medium-sized saucepan and vegetable oil on a moderate flame.
4. Cook for another few minutes after adding the omelet ingredients.
5. Flip the omelet over using a spatula and immediately turn off the heat when it's almost done cooking. Top with some bonito flakes, grated daikon, & a splash of soy sauce on a serving dish to complete the recipe. Serve right away.

NUTRITION

Calories 153 Kcal | fat 12 g |
Carbohydrate 4 g |
Protein 9 g

KINAKO DANGO

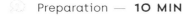

Preparation — **10 MIN**

Cook Time — **4 MIN**

Servings — **4**

INGREDIENTS

- 1 cup rice flour dango powder
- ½ cup of icy water
- ½ cup of kinako
- 2 tbsp sugar granulated
- ½ tsp kosher salt

NUTRITION

Calories 406 Kcal | fat 2 g |
Carbohydrate 90 g |
Protein 7 g

INSTRUCTIONS

1. Bring a large pot of boiling water to a rolling boil on the stovetop.
2. Add the dango powder & water to a small bowl and whisk to combine. It's time to get down to business!
3. A little amount of dough should be formed into a bite-size ball. Repeat this process until all of the dough is gone.
4. Prepare a bowl of ice water in advance.
5. Pour boiling water over Dango balls till they float to the surface. Add chilled water to the drained water. Allow them to cool & drain for three minutes.
6. Toss the kinako with the salt and sugar in a separate bowl and thoroughly combine the ingredients. Serve the kinako mix with Dango balls & the rest of the kinako. Serve.

DORAYAKI PANCAKES WITH BEAN PASTE

Preparation — **5 MIN**

Cook Time — **6 MIN**

Servings — **4**

INGREDIENTS

- 3 eggs large
- ¼ cup sugar granulated
- 3 tbsp of honey
- 2 cups of all-purpose flour
- 1 tsp powder baking
- 2 tbsp water
- for frying vegetable oil
- Anko

INSTRUCTIONS

1. Add sugar and honey to a bowl and whisk until smooth.
2. Mix the flour & baking powder in a separate bowl.
3. While mixing the egg & sugar mixture, gradually add the flour and water. The batter must be thick yet pourable (and not very sticky).
4. Use a cotton towel to wipe away any excess oil from the pan. Because we want the pancakes to have a consistent brown hue, we need to use small oil in the pan.
5. Reduce the heat to low and swirl the pan as you gently pour in 3 tbsp of batter.
6. To create more pancakes, use a pan that can handle more than one at a time.
7. Immediately after the pancake begins to bubble, turn it over & cook for a further 2 to 3 minutes on the second side. Repeat this process until all of the batters have been utilized.
8. Take a pancake and a couple of tsp of Anko and put it on it. Place a second pancake on top and keep warm. Continue this process until you've used up all of the pancakes. Serve.

NUTRITION

Calories 366 Kcal | fat 4 g |
Carbohydrate 74 g |
Protein 10 g

SPINACH SALAD WITH GINGER-SOY

Preparation — **5 MIN**

Cook Time — **15 MIN**

Servings — **4**

INGREDIENTS

- 3 tbsp onion minced
- 3 tbsp canola oil or peanut
- 2 tbsp white vinegar distilled
- 1 & ½ tbsp fresh ginger finely grated
- 1 tbsp ketchup
- 1 tbsp soy sauce reduced-sodium
- ¼ tsp garlic minced
- ¼ tsp salt
- pepper Freshly ground
- 1 large, grated carrot
- 1 red thinly sliced bell pepper medium
- 10 oz spinach fresh

INSTRUCTIONS

1. A food processor or blender works well for blending the ingredients listed above. Take a blender or food processor and blitz until smooth.
2. Combine the spinach, carrots, and bell peppers with the dressing in a medium bowl.

NUTRITION

Calories 135 Kcal | fat 11 g |
Carbohydrate 9 g |
Protein 3 g

SMOKED SALMON MAKI ROLLS

Preparation — **5 MIN**

Cook Time — **5 MIN**

Servings — **1**

INGREDIENTS

- 1 nori seaweed sheet toasted
- 1 oz salmon smoked
- 4 avocado slices
- ¼ cup carrot shredded
- 4 thin cucumber strips

INSTRUCTIONS

1. The shiny side of nori should be facing up.
2. Then, on the bottom 3rd of nori, arrange the avocado, carrots, salmon, and cucumbers.
3. Seal your nori roll by moistening the final inch of a roll. Slice into eight pieces. Serve and enjoy!

NUTRITION

Calories 130 Kcal | fat 9 g |
Carbohydrate 8 g |
Protein 7 g

CRISPY FRIED PORK BOWL

Preparation — **25 MIN**

Cook Time — **7 MIN**

Servings — **2**

INGREDIENTS

- 2/3 cup dashi stock prepared
- 2 tsp sugar white
- 2 tsp mirin (sweet wine Japanese)
- 2 tsp sauce soy
- ½ tsp salt
- 1 tbsp oil vegetable
- 1 chopped small onion
- 2 (3 oz) pork chops fried breaded
- 2 beaten eggs
- 1 & ½ cups short-grain rice cooked

INSTRUCTIONS

1. Combine the dashi, soy sauce, sugar, mirin, and salt in a mixing bowl.
2. In a medium skillet set over medium heat, warm the vegetable oil.
3. Add the onion and simmer, often stirring, for 5 minutes or until transparent. Add the dashi mixture to the mixture and stir. Place pig pieces over top of onions in an orderly manner. Slices should be drizzled with beaten eggs.
4. Cook the eggs in a covered skillet for 2 minutes or until they are set.
5. Rice should be served in two separate containers, one for each person. Top each with half of the eggs, onions, and pork pieces.

NUTRITION

Calories 590 Kcal | fat 24 g |
Carbohydrate 58 g |
Protein 32 g

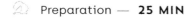

CALI ROLLS CON MANGO E MAYO

Preparation — **30 MIN**

Cook Time — **40 MIN**

Servings — **4**

INGREDIENTS

- Rice
- 1 &1/3 cups rinsed black rice
- 2 & 2/3 cups of water
- 2 tbsp vinegar rice
- 1 tbsp sugar
- ¾ tsp salt kosher
- Rolls
- 4 nori sheets
- 4 tsp seeds sesame
- 1 sliced Persian cucumber
- ½ sliced ripe mango
- ¾ medium sliced ripe avocado
- 1 cup drained lump crabmeat
- 1/3 cup wasabi mayonnaise or Sriracha

NUTRITION

Calories 500 Kcal | fat 23 g | Carbohydrate 58 g | Protein 21 g

INSTRUCTIONS

1. In a small saucepan, combine the rice & water, then bring to a boil. Bring to the boil. Continue cooking until the water has been absorbed & rice is soft, then remove the lid. Allow cooling for ten minutes after removing from heat.
2. Put sugar & salt in a microwave-safe bowl with vinegar & microwave for 30 seconds. Microwave on High for approximately 30 seconds till the sugar & salt are dissolved. Fluff your rice using a fork after adding the ingredients. Set on a baking pan and wait for it to cool completely before handling.
3. Rolls may be made as follows: You may use plastic wrap to protect a bamboo sushi mat. A nori sheet should be placed on the mat, with its shiny side facing down. Rice is distributed and pressed onto nori with your moist fingertips. Add 1 tbsp of sesame seeds to the top.
4. Turn the nori over so that the rice side faces the plastic wrap and enjoy the fresh taste of sushi. The bottom 3rd of the shiny side of nori should be covered with one-fourth of cucumber, avocado, mango, and crab.
5. To seal the nori roll, soak the final inch of nori with the mat before rolling it up securely. Use a mat to form the roll by pressing it firmly with your hands.
6. To create 3 additional rolls, repeat the process with the remaining components.
7. It is best to use a knife and a moist cloth to cut every roll into eight pieces. Mayonnaise should be sprinkled on top.

CHICKEN KATSU WITH CREAMY SLAW

Preparation — **10 MIN**

Cook Time — **30 MIN**

Servings — **4**

INGREDIENTS

- 4 chicken thighs boneless, skinless
- ¼ tsp salt
- ¼ tsp pepper ground
- 3 tbsp flour all-purpose
- 1 large beaten egg
- 1 cup breadcrumbs panko
- 5 tbsp grapeseed or peanut oil
- 4 sliced scallions
- 1 tbsp fresh ginger minced
- 6 cups red cabbage thinly sliced
- ½ cup carrot grated
- 2 tbsp mayonnaise
- 2 tbsp soy sauce reduced-sodium
- 2 tbsp vinegar rice
- 1 tsp sugar white

NUTRITION

Calories 539 Kcal | fat 34 g | Carbohydrate 26 g | Protein 33 g

INSTRUCTIONS

1. In between two sheets of plastic wrap, place the chicken. A heavy skillet or meat mallet with a smooth surface is ideal for this step. Salt & pepper to taste. Put the flour, the egg, and the panko into three shallow plates.
2. Before coating with panko, dredge your chicken into flour and shake off any excess.
3. Next, dab it in an egg and allow any excess drop-off.
4. In a large skillet, heat 1 tbsp of oil over medium-high heat. Reduce the heat to medium-low, add half your chicken, & cook for 3-4 minutes, or until the chicken is golden brown.
5. Incorporate 1 tbsp of oil into the chicken by turning it over. Cook for a further 3-4 minutes, or till golden brown & cooked through on the opposite side.
6. Wrap the chicken in Al foil and place it on a serving platter. A total of 2 tbsp of oil and the leftover chicken should be used in this process again. The pan has to be cleaned.
7. In the same pan, heat oil to medium heat. Stir in the scallions & ginger for around 30 seconds.
8. Add your cabbage, carrots, and heat, often turning, for 1–2 minutes or until cabbage begins to wilt. Removing the food from the heat is necessary.
9. A medium quantity of mayonnaise is needed to make this dressing. Toss within cabbage mixture & stir well until it's evenly distributed.
10. Serve your chicken & slaw together.

RENKON CHIPS

Preparation — **5 MIN**

Cook Time — **10 MIN**

Servings — **1**

INGREDIENTS

- 250g frozen lotus roots sliced Renkon
- deep fry Oil
- Shichimi Togarashi Pinch

Amazu Sauce

- 1 tbs sauce soy
- 1 tbs sake
- 1 tbs sugar
- 1 tbs mirin
- ½ tbs vinegar rice
- 1 tbs water

NUTRITION

Calories 288 Kcal | fat 3 g |
Carbohydrate 65 g |
Protein 1 g

INSTRUCTIONS

1. Sliced renkon may be defrosted on the paper towel and let absorb the water.
2. More paper towels may be used to remove any remaining water.
3. Allow the oil to reach 180 degrees Fahrenheit before frying the sliced renkon.
4. Deep-fry the sliced renkon for approximately five minutes or until gently browned. The renkon will have many bubbles surrounding it. It's ready to scrape out of oil when the renkon stops creating bubbles around it and becomes brown.
5. When draining, use a paper towel to absorb any remaining oil.
6. Pour Amazu sauce over the dish & sprinkle Shichimi togarashi on top.

AMAZU SAUCE

7. Add the ingredients to a small saucepan and bring to a boil.
8. Bring your sauce mix to a boil in a medium saucepan over high heat.
9. Bring to a simmer over medium heat.
10. Once the sauce has thickened and decreased in volume, remove it from the heat.
11. Drizzle it over renkon chips using a sauce dispenser.

EASY JAPANESE FRIED RICE

Preparation — **5 MIN**

Cook Time — **10 MIN**

Servings — **2**

INGREDIENTS

- 2 rice bowls of short-grain rice cooked in Japanese
- 2 ham slices
- 1 green scallion/onion
- 1 egg large
- 2 Tbsp oil neutral-flavored
- ½ tsp sea salt or kosher
- 1/8 tsp pepper powder white
- 2 tsp sauce soy

NUTRITION

Calories 318 Kcal | fat 19 g | Carbohydrate 28 g | Protein 9 g

INSTRUCTIONS

1. To reheat day-old cooked rice, take the rice out of the fridge and microwave it until it reaches room temperature. Transfer the heated rice to the baking sheet if you're using two servings of cooked rice. Allow it to cool fully on a flat surface. The rice will get drier as a result of this.
2. The white portion of a green onion should be cut into rounds, while the green section should be sliced in half. Different the white & green components and place them in a separate location. Keep green slices on hand for sprinkling on top.
3. Slice the ham into 12-inch (1.3-centimeter) squares. Crack an egg into a bowl & whisk it.

TO COOK THE FRIED RICE

4. Make sure you have all ingredients ready to go before cooking this recipe. In a big frying pan, heat the wok to medium-high heat. Swirl in half of the oil once it's heated, and make sure it's covered the whole wok's surface! Heat a wok and add the egg to it. The egg will begin to rise to the surface of the oil after a few seconds.
5. Swirl your loosely cooked egg in the pan with the blunt end of the spatula to keep everything fluffy while it cooks.
6. Using a slotted spoon, carefully lift out the egg from the pan when the bottom is set; however, the peak is still runny & not cooked. At this point, we wouldn't like to overcook your egg.

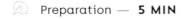

7. Add the rest of the oil to a pan and stir it around. Ham and diced green onion should then be added. Add the oil and cook until well-coated.
8. Add the rice to a wok when it has cooled down. Separate your rice clumps using a spatula in a slicing motion, so don't smash or break the rice grains. Add the ham combination & continue to stir the rice until it is covered in oil & has a good sear on the outside.
9. While stirring the rice, return the scrambled egg to the pan and break it into smaller pieces. If you're utilizing nonstick wok, you'll be able to simply remove any rice that becomes stuck to the pan. This imparts a smoky taste. You might add additional oil with a steel pan because the rice sticks more. Salt and pepper the rice to taste.
10. Toss in the soy sauce to evenly coat the rice. The idea here is to avoid the fried rice from clumping by constantly tossing it in the air rather than leaving it as a sticky mass at the base of the pan. Adding a smokey taste to the rice is easier by turning and tossing it.
11. Add your chopped green onion green portion. If necessary, season the fried rice to taste. Transfer the rice to a serving dish after tossing it a couple more times.
12. To Serve, it's fairly uncommon for Japanese Chinese restaurants to offer fried rice in a dome form. Fill the rice bowl with fried rice, press it gently to compact it, then invert this onto a platter if you'd want to serve it this way. The rice dish should be refilled for the second plate. Sliced green onion may be sprinkled over the top.
13. To Store, you may keep any leftovers in the fridge for up to two days or in the freezer for up to a month if sealed tightly.

YAKI ONIGIRI

Preparation — **15 MIN**

Cook Time — **15 MIN**

Servings — **4**

INGREDIENTS

- For Making Rice
- 2 cups of short-grain rice uncooked Japanese
- 400ml water
- For Cooking Yaki Ongiri
- 1 Tbsp Sea salt or kosher
- 1 Tbsp oil neutral-flavored
- soy sauce

NUTRITION

Calories 147 Kcal | fat 1 g | Carbohydrate 31 g | Protein 3 g

INSTRUCTIONS

1. Make a list of everything you need. You may use a rice cooker, a saucepan on the stove, or an instant pot to prepare the rice for your meal. Let the rice cool down a little before handling it to don't burn your hands. The rice should not be allowed to cool fully.

TO MAKE RICE BALLS

2. First, moisten the hands using water to prevent the rice from sticking.
3. Then, smear it all over using your hands and a little salt.
4. You'll need a half-cup of rice for this.
5. Gently shape the rice in a triangle by covering it with your other hand.
6. Make sure the hand covering you (in this case, my right hand) forms a triangle. You need to keep your hands just firm enough to keep the shape of the onigiri from breaking apart as you construct it. Avoid squeezing the rice too hard.
7. Cover the region with an index finger, thumb, and middle finger to create a neat triangular form. Make an excellent triangle by rotating the onigiri.
8. To maintain a decent shape, you must press onigiri with one hand while firmly squeezing them.
9. On both edges of the triangle, gently compress the center of the triangle to create a small depression. It's time for onigiri! It doesn't

matter how long I've been practicing; you can still tell I'm not a decent onigiri maker.

TO GRILL RICE BALL

10. Heat a medium-sized cast-iron pan with a little oil.

11. Crispy & lightly browned onigiri is ready to be served. When the rice has a good crust, it will release itself. Don't make a hasty flip. Take your time and just work on a side to prevent it from splitting into pieces.

12. Lower the heat to medium-low after the bread has browned and toasted to your liking. Apply soy sauce on all surfaces. Ensure that all food is cooked evenly by rotating the pan many times. After brushing onigiri with sauce, take care not to burn it.

To Store : When rice is refrigerated, it becomes brittle. Yaki Onigiri keeps well within the refrigerator for two days when wrapped in plastic wrap and covered with a heavy kitchen towel. Using a towel to protect the rice from becoming too cold and the meal excessively cold is a great idea. Reheat in the frying pan or microwave when you're ready to dine on the food.

MISO GLAZED SALMON

Preparation — **15 MIN**

Cook Time — **12 MIN**

Servings — **2**

INGREDIENTS

- 2 fillets Salmon
- 1 tsp salt

Miso Glaze

- 3 tbsp awase or miso white
- 3 tbsp sugar
- 1 tbsp mirin
- 1 tbsp sake

NUTRITION

Calories 384 Kcal | fat 12 g |
Carbohydrate 29 g |
Protein 37 g

INSTRUCTIONS

1. Cover your salmon fillets using cling wrap & let them sit for around 15 minutes before sprinkling them with salt.
2. With the kitchen towel, remove any extra moisture from the fish.
3. These ingredients should be combined in the Ziplock bag before being sealed.
4. The package should include two salmon fillets. Close the bag and use your hand to brush the salmon with the miso marinade.
5. Refrigerate the marinate for at least 7-8 hours.
6. Remove any remaining miso marinade from the meat using a kitchen paper towel.
7. To bake the salmon, place it on the baking sheet that has been coated with Al foil.
8. In the oven's bottom row, the salmon should be grilled/broiled for 6 minutes at 410°F.
9. After 6 minutes in the oven, flip the salmon over & cook for an additional 3 minutes.
10. Turn it over, spray it with miso marinade, and then put it back in the oven for a minute to finish cooking.
11. The glazed salmon is best served over soba noodles or rice with a side of vegetables.
12. Toast the sesame seeds & finely cut the coarsely diced green shallots for garnish.

ASIAN SLAW

Preparation — **10 MIN**

Cook Time — **5 MIN**

Servings — **4**

INGREDIENTS

Sesame Soy Dressings

- 2 tbsp rice vinegar
- ½ tbsp soy sauce
- ½ tbsp mirin
- 1 tbsp honey
- ½ tsp ginger grated
- ½ tbsp olive oil
- ½ tbsp seeds oil sesame
- ½ tbsp seeds sesame

Asian Slaw

- 50g red cabbage
- 50g green cabbage
- 1 scallion
- 50g Napa cabbage
- ½ carrot
- ¼ cup frozen edamame
- garnish Watercress
- 2 tbsp garnish fried noodle

NUTRITION

Calories 84 Kcal | fat 5 g |
Carbohydrate 10 g |
Protein 2 g

INSTRUCTIONS

SESAME SOY DRESSINGS

1. Combine all your ingredients & set them aside.

ASIAN SLAW

2. Shred the red, napa, green, and carrots finely.
3. Set aside finely chopped scallion.
4. Rinse the shredded veggies in a large running water bowl to remove dirt or debris.
5. Drain the water out using a sieve.
6. Remove as much water as possible from the shredded veggies by spinning them in a salad spinner.
7. Put the veggies on a serving dish and serve immediately.
8. Serve with watercress and crispy noodles on the side. Serve with some sesame & soy dressings.

GYUDON JAPANESE BEEF BOWLS

Preparation — **5 MIN**

Cook Time — **10 MIN**

Servings — **2**

INGREDIENTS

- 150 g beef thinly sliced
- ½ onion
- 1 tbsp ginger red pickled
- 1 tbsp diagonally & scallion thinly sliced
- 3 cups Japanese rice cooked
- ½ tbsp oil olive

Sauce

- 200ml water
- 1 tsp powder dashi
- 2 tsp sugar
- 1 tbsp sake
- 1 tbsp mirin
- 1 tsp juice of ginger
- 2 tbsp sauce soy

INSTRUCTIONS

1. Using a sharp knife, cut the onion in half.
2. Cook your onion in a little olive oil into a skillet on medium heat until translucent.
3. Add all of the sauce ingredients after the onion is transparent.
4. In a medium saucepan, bring the water to a boil, lower the heat & simmer for approximately 5 minutes.
5. Remove the pan from the heat after the steak is done & the sauce thickens a little.
6. Served with steamed rice and some scallions & ginger pickles on the side.

NUTRITION

Calories 667 Kcal | fat 20 g | Carbohydrate 93 g | Protein 22 g

YAKIMESHI / JAPANESE FRIED RICE

Preparation — **10 MIN**

Cook Time — **10 MIN**

Servings — **4**

INGREDIENTS

- 2 cups rice cooked
- 2 tbsp Mayonnaise Kewpie Japanese
- 2 slices of bacon
- 2 large eggs
- ¼ cup shallots green
- ½ tsp salt
- to taste Pepper

INSTRUCTIONS

1. In a mixing bowl, combine the mayonnaise and the cooked rice.
2. Trim and finely chop some green shallots & the bacon.
3. Add the rice to a hot frying pan with a drizzle of olive oil and cook for a few minutes, stirring occasionally.
4. Add eggs & scramble them solely on a single side of the pan while the rice cooks on the other.
5. After half of the egg has been fried, add it to the rice. About 5 minutes later, add the bacon. Then add the salt & the shallots and mix.
6. Immediately remove the food from the fire and sprinkle it with a little pepper.

NUTRITION

Calories 183 Kcal | fat 7 g | Carbohydrate 22 g | Protein 5 g

SHRIMP FRIED RICE W/ YUM SAUCE

Preparation — **15 MIN**

Cook Time — **35 MIN**

Servings — **6**

INGREDIENTS

- 2 cups jasmine rice uncooked
- 3 cups of water
- 3 tbsp divided vegetable oil
- 1 chopped sweet onion
- 2 crushed & minced cloves of garlic
- 1 package of peas & carrots frozen
- 4 tbsp divided butter
- 2 large eggs
- 4 tbsp sauce oyster
- 3 tbsp sauce soy
- 1 juiced, divided lemon
- to taste salt & pepper
- 1 lb uncooked peeled & deveined medium shrimp
- Yum Sauce:
- 1 cup of mayonnaise
- 3 tbsp water
- 2 tbsp paprika
- 1 tsp paste ginger
- 1 tsp sugar white
- ½ tsp powder garlic
- to taste salt & pepper

NUTRITION

Calories 785 Kcal | fat 47 g | Carbohydrate 70 g | Protein 23 g

INSTRUCTIONS

1. In a pot, combine 3 cups of water and rice and bring to a boil.
2. Simmer for 20 to 25 minutes, with the heat reduced to medium-low and the lid on, until the rice is cooked and the liquid has evaporated. Allow cooling before moving on to the next step.
3. Heat 2 tbsp of vegetable oil over medium-high heat in a large, deep pan. Add the onion and simmer for 5 minutes, or until tender and transparent.
4. Add garlic and simmer for a minute or so until it's fragrant. Sauté for 5 minutes or until the rice starts to brown, then add in frozen peas-carrots combination and stir well.
5. Toss in 2 Tbsp of butter and mix until smooth. Cook the eggs until they are set, then remove from heat. Soy sauce, Oyster sauce, and half a lemon juice should be added and stirred into the mixture. Use salt and pepper to taste.
6. Heat the remaining 1 tbsp of vegetable oil in a separate pan to medium-high heat. Add the

shrimp and cook for 2-3 mins, or until they are pink on the outside and opaque in the middle. Add the remaining 2 tbsp. Butter and lemon juice and combine well. The fried rice mixture should be added to this mixture.

7. Yuzu sauce is made by mixing mayonnaise with various ingredients, including paprika, white sugar, ginger paste, and salt & pepper. Make sure everything is fully combined. The fried rice goes well with this dish.

SOBA NOODLE VEGGIE BOWL

Preparation — **15 MIN**

Cook Time — **10 MIN**

Servings — **1**

INGREDIENTS

- 3 oz soba noodles dried
- 2 tbsp sauce soy
- 2 tbsp sauce oyster
- 1 tbsp mirin (sweet wine Japanese)
- 1 tbsp olive oil
- ½ green chopped bell pepper
- ¼ sliced onion
- ½ cup trimmed green beans fresh
- 1 cup spinach leaves baby

NUTRITION

Calories 503 Kcal | fat 14 g | Carbohydrate 81 g | Protein 17 g

INSTRUCTIONS

1. Bring a large saucepan of lightly salted water to a rolling boil, then remove from the heat. Adding soba noodles once the water returns to a boil completes the preparation.

2. Using an uncovered pan, cook for approximately 7 minutes, turning periodically until the vegetables are cooked but still firm to the biting. Drain.

3. To make the sauces, in a mixing bowl, mix the oyster sauce, soy sauce, & mirin until well combined. Remove from consideration.

4. In a pan, heat the olive oil at medium heat. Toss in the vegetables and cook for 2-3 mins, depending on how soft or crisp you like your vegetables.

5. Toss in the cooked soba noodles and veggies before serving. Add the soy sauce mixture and simmer for 1-2 minutes, stirring often.

6. After 2-3 mins, add the baby spinach and simmer for another 2 minutes. Serve in a dish.

CRISPY FRIED PORK CUTLETS

Preparation — **5 MIN**

Cook Time — **20 MIN**

Servings — **4**

INGREDIENTS

- 2 trimmed pork chops boneless
- ½ tsp salt
- ¼ tsp black pepper ground
- 1 large egg
- ½ tsp soy sauce
- ¼ cup flour all-purpose
- ½ cup bread crumbs panko
- Oil for frying

NUTRITION

Calories 322 Kcal | fat 26 g | Carbohydrate 16 g | Protein 10 g

INSTRUCTIONS

1. Paper towels may absorb any extra moisture from pork chops before cooking. Salt & pepper to taste.
2. In a mixing bowl, combine the egg & soy sauce.
3. Mix flour and panko into a small bowl. Use your fingers to massage the flour into all of the nooks and crannies of the pork chop. All sides should be coated uniformly.
4. Dip the pork within the egg mixture until it is thoroughly covered. Panko-coating should be done shortly after transfer to the panko. Perform the same procedure a second time with the remaining pork chop.
5. 350 degrees Fahrenheit should be the oil temperature in a large pan or wok. Fry the pork chop inside a skillet over medium heat. 2–3 minutes on the bottom side should do the trick. After 2-3 mins on the second side, the pork should be golden brown, and the middle should still be pink. Insert an instant-read thermometer into the middle, and the reading should be at least 145 degrees F.
6. Allow the oil to drip off the cutlet by holding onto its edge for another few seconds. Let it dry on a piece of paper.
7. Repeat this process with the other pork chop.

CHICKEN YAKISOBA

Preparation — **20 MIN**

Cook Time — **15 MIN**

Servings — **4**

INGREDIENTS

- 2/3 cup dashi stock prepared
- 2 tsp sugar white
- 2 tsp mirin (sweet wine Japanese)
- 2 tsp sauce soy
- ½ tsp salt
- 1 tbsp oil vegetable
- 1 chopped small onion
- 2 (3 oz) pork chops fried breaded
- 2 beaten eggs
- 1 & ½ cups short-grain rice cooked

INSTRUCTIONS

1. Sesame oil & canola oil in a big pan over medium-high heat are also good choices. Stir-fry the chicken & garlic in a little heated oil for a minute until aromatic. Add chili paste to the mixture and simmer for another 3-4 minutes when the chicken is browned. Two minutes later, add the soy sauce & continue cooking. In a large bowl, combine the chicken with the marinade.

2. This recipe uses canola oil & 3-4 minutes of stirring to cook and wilt a head of cabbage in a pan.

3. Combine the chicken and cabbage and stir well. Adding noodles, cook & toss until the noodles become hot and the chicken isn't any longer pink inside, about 3-4 minutes, then serve. Pickled ginger may be added to the dish as a finishing touch.

NUTRITION

Calories 503 Kcal | fat 17 g |
Carbohydrate 70 g |
Protein 27 g

SESAME CHICKEN AND SOBA NOODLES

Preparation — **10 MIN**

Cook Time — **15 MIN**

Servings — **4**

INGREDIENTS

- 1 package of soba noodles dried
- 3 tbsp sauce soy
- 3 tbsp sugar brown
- 1 lb chicken breasts, boneless, skinless cubed
- 2 tbsp seeds sesame
- ½ cup of oil olive
- 3 tbsp vinegar rice
- 1 tbsp ginger finely grated
- 1 package of salad greens mixed

INSTRUCTIONS

1. Bring a saucepan of salted water to your rolling boil, then remove it from the heat.
2. Add soba noodles to the boiling water, lower the heat and simmer for a few minutes. The noodles should be soft yet firm to bite when cooked for 5-7 minutes with the lid off and stirring now and then.
3. Drain and run cold water over the whole area.
4. In a medium pan, combine soy sauce & brown sugar, then warm over medium heat.
5. Chicken cubes should no longer be pink in the middle, and the fluids should flow clear, around 5-7 minutes. Toss with sesame seeds in a bowl to combine.
6. To make the vinaigrette, put the vinegar, olive oil, and ginger in a bowl.
7. Assemble four dishes of greens and top with some soba noodle salad and chicken.
8. Dress the salad with a vinaigrette before serving.

NUTRITION

Calories 635 Kcal | fat 33 g |
Carbohydrate 56 g |
Protein 34 g

OMELETTE FOR LEFTOVERS

Preparation — **10 MIN**

Cook Time — **25 MIN**

Servings — **1**

INGREDIENTS

- 1 & ½ tsp butter
- 1 small, sliced tomato
- ½ red sliced bell pepper
- ¼ sliced onion
- ¼ sliced zucchini
- 1 oz mushrooms sliced
- ½ cup cooked rice warm
- 1 tbsp ketchup
- 1 slice chopped cooked bacon
- ½ tsp paprika
- salt and black pepper ground
- 2 lightly beaten eggs

NUTRITION

Calories 369 Kcal | fat 17 g |
Carbohydrate 43 g |
Protein 19 g

INSTRUCTIONS

1. Over medium-low heat, melt the butter in a skillet. This recipe calls for 5 minutes of cooking time for the vegetables to soften before serving.
2. Toss the rice with ketchup, bacon, paprika, salt, & black pepper. Serve on a serving dish.
3. Over medium-high heat, place a nonstick skillet. Eggs should be spread out in a light coating and cooked for around 5 minutes.
4. Eggs may be served on top of the rice.

OKONOMIYAKI WITH PRAWNS

Preparation — **10 MIN**

Cook Time — **15 MIN**

Servings — **4**

INGREDIENTS

- 1 & ½ cups flour plain
- 1 tsp powder baking
- 4 lightly beaten eggs
- 2 tbsp miso paste white
- 1 cup soda water cold
- ¼ finely shredded white cabbage
- 1 coarsely grated zucchini
- 3 long thinly sliced green shallots
- 20 medium peeled, deveined green prawns
- 1/3 cup oil sunflower

INSTRUCTIONS

1. In a medium bowl, whisk together the flour & baking powder. Gently whisk the soda water to produce a smooth batter by making a well in the middle of the dry ingredients. Stir in the prawns, veggies, and seasonings before serving. Season.

2. Heat 1 tbsp of oil over medium heat in a large frying pan. Pour ¼ cup (60 ml) of batter for every pancake into the pan & cook for around 4 minutes, or until golden & cooked through, working in batches. Serve immediately or cover with foil and reheat in the oven if desired. Replicate with the leftover batter and oil.

3. Onion rings, avocado slices, sesame seeds, & long green shallots are needed to accompany this okonomiyaki dish.

NUTRITION

Calories 400 Kcal | fat 5 g |
Carbohydrate 92 g |
Protein 10 g

JAPANESE MOUNTAIN YAM (NAGAIMO) SALAD

Preparation — **10 MIN**

Cook Time — **0 MIN**

Servings — **2**

INGREDIENTS

- 1 nagaimo small piece
- bonito flakes Dried
- Daikon sprouts, thinly sliced kaiware, leaves green perilla

INSTRUCTIONS

1. Amass the necessary components.
2. Remove the nagaimo's outer skin with a vegetable peeler to reveal the white interior meat of the root. The yam's slick feel results from its mucilaginous texture, making it difficult to handle.
3. Cut the nagaimo into tiny, thin rectangles by slicing it lengthwise. Chill within the refrigerator till ready to be served on separate appetizer plates.
4. Garnish using dry bonito flakes and shiso, daikon sprouts, or other additional garnishes just before you serve it. Pour some soy sauce on top or season it by using soy sauce.

NUTRITION

Calories 09 Kcal | fat 0 g |
Carbohydrate 02 g |
Protein 0 g

SPICY KONNYAKU / JAPANESE YAM CAKE

Preparation — **10 MIN**

Cook Time — **10 MIN**

Servings — **4**

INGREDIENTS

- 1 package yam cake Japanese konnyaku
- 2 tbsp of water, or dashi katsuo bonito
- 3 tsp soy sauce dashi-seasoned
- 1-2 tsp soy sauce
- 1/8 tsp 7-chile pepper Japanese, shichimi togarashi

INSTRUCTIONS

1. Konnyaku may be sliced into matchsticks or any other desired shape or size.
2. Use a medium-sized nonstick frying pan to heat the ingredients. Konnyaku and water should be added to the mixture. Keep the mixture constantly moving.
3. Stir in the 7-chili pepper and cook until the liquid has almost evaporated 6-8 minutes. Add extra soy sauce if necessary.
4. Serve the spiciness of the konnyaku on tiny plates after it has been removed from the heat. Add an extra 7-chile pepper to the dish.

NUTRITION

Calories 184 Kcal | fat 3 g | Carbohydrate 37 g | Protein 3 g

NATTO WITH RICE

Preparation — **5 MIN**

Cook Time — **5 MIN**

Servings — **1**

INGREDIENTS

- 1 cup of cooked white rice short-grain
- 2 packets of soybeans fermented
- 1 tsp sauce soy

NUTRITION

Calories 419 Kcal | fat 11 g | Carbohydrate 57 g | Protein 24 g

INSTRUCTIONS

1. Make a big dish of hot cooked rice. Combine 2 natto packets in a mixing bowl. Add all ingredients of the seasoning sauce & karashi sachets that came with the box to the bowl. Chopsticks are a good tool for mixing forcefully.
2. Add your favorite toppings to the natto, if desired. Individual preferences may need the use of more soy sauce. All of the garnishes, as mentioned above, may be used in any combination.
3. Add additional toppings as desired to the steaming rice before serving.

JAPANESE DYNAMITE APPETIZERS

Preparation — **15 MIN**

Cook Time — **15 MIN**

Servings — **18**

INGREDIENTS

- 1 bag mixed seafood frozen
- 1 package button mushrooms white, stems removed & sliced
- 1 cup of light mayonnaise
- 2 tbsp Masago caviar

INSTRUCTIONS

1. The oven should be preheated at 375 degrees Fahrenheit. Aluminum foil cups should be used to line a muffin tray.
2. Seafood should be simmered for about 10 mins or until it's cooked through in a medium saucepan of water brought to a boil. Drain and let it cool down a little before serving.
3. Drain any extra liquid from the mushrooms before sautéing them for best results.
4. Once at room temperature, drain the mushrooms and dry them using paper towels.
5. Mix the cooked seafood, mayonnaise, mushrooms, & masago in a separate bowl. Gently blend all ingredients until well combined.
6. Scoop a tiny amount into each of the Al foil cups with care.
7. Tops of dynamite should be browned in about 15 minutes. For a darker brown on the tops, put the oven broiler on for the last 2-3 mins of baking.
8. Add a little more masago on the rims of every dynamite cup before serving.

NUTRITION

Calories 57 Kcal | fat 3 g | Carbohydrate 2 g | Protein 5 g

PORK GYOZA

Preparation — **20 MIN**

Cook Time — **20 MIN**

Servings — **8**

INGREDIENTS

- ¾ cup Napa cabbage shredded
- ½ lb pork ground
- 1 medium diced green onion
- 2 tsp ginger minced
- 1 lightly beaten large egg
- 1 tbsp sauce soy
- ¼ tsp chili oil hot
- ¼ tsp oil sesame
- 2 tbsp oil vegetable
- 30 wrappers gyoza

INSTRUCTIONS

1. Boiled water with salt is ready for use. 3–to 5 minutes of blanching the shredded cabbage are plenty.
2. Squeeze off any remaining water from the cooked cabbage after being plunged into an ice bath to halt the cooking process.
3. Prepared cabbage, pork & other ingredients in a small bowl. Add the minced ginger & soy sauces, along with the chili oil & sesame oil, to taste. To assemble, stir the ingredients together until well combined.
4. In front of you, place a gyoza wrapper. Apply water to all of the edges. In the center of the wrapper, place a spoonful of the filling.
5. Make a semicircle by folding the sides in and pinching the edges together. Create pleats if needed. Continue making gyoza until all of the fillings have been used up.
6. Preheat a heavy nonstick frying pan on medium heat to prepare the food with 1 tbsp of olive oil. Stack 12-15 gyoza and fry for 2 mins, or until they're browned on the bottom.
7. To a pan, add water. Cook your dumplings with the lid unless the water has been absorbed, then remove from heat. Repeat the process with the remaining gyozas.

NUTRITION

Calories 131 Kcal | fat 6 g |
Carbohydrate 13 g |
Protein 6 g

IKA / TEMPURA SQUID

Preparation — **20 MIN**

Cook Time — **5 MIN**

Servings — **4**

INGREDIENTS

- 1 lb squid, cleaned body only
- ¾ cup flour all-purpose
- ¼ cup starch potato
- 1 egg large
- ¾ cup water ice-cold
- for frying Canola oil
- ¼ tsp shichimi togarashi, 7-spice chili Japanese pepper
- ¼ tsp aonori, Japanese seaweed flakes green
- to taste Salt

NUTRITION

Calories 617 Kcal | fat 31 g | Carbohydrate 64 g | Protein 20 g

INSTRUCTIONS

1. Slice the cleaned squid shell into rings. If you're using fresh squid, cut it into ¼-inch rings; otherwise, thaw frozen calamari rings.
2. Oil should be heated to 350-360 degrees Fahrenheit in a wide medium pan.
3. Make your tempura batter while the oil is heating. Mix flour & potato starch in a medium-sized bowl and stir to combine. Shimmering seven-spice chili pepper and Aomori are added to the tempura batter, then gently mixed in.
4. Using a large measuring cup, combine the egg with the cold water until the mixture measures 1 cup. Make sure you don't over-mix the egg & water by gently incorporating them.
5. Take a spoon and gently stir in the wet components with the dry ones. Make sure you don't overwork the batter, which will make it harder and chewier.
6. You need to work as soon as you get the tempura batter out of the fridge. Instead of dipping every calamari ring one at a time into the batter, consider swiftly moving many rings to the heated oil & dipping them all at once.
7. Fry them for 30 to 40 seconds, or until they're a light gold color. A minute or two in the oil is all it takes to cook them.
8. Allow your ika-furai to dry on paper towels, then sprinkle it with salt to your preference.
9. Sprinkle on more shichimi togarashi & aonori for more flavor.

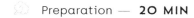

JAPANESE STEAMED PORK

Preparation — **15 MIN**

Cook Time — **15 MIN**

Servings — **4**

INGREDIENTS

- ¾ lb ground pork lean
- 3 mushrooms shiitake, dried or fresh
- 1 tbsp garlic chopped
- 1 onion green
- 1 tsp fresh ginger grated or chopped
- 1 tbsp sauce soy
- 2 tbsp sake
- 1 tsp sesame oil
- ¼-1/3 tsp salt
- 1/8 tsp black pepper freshly ground
- 2 tbsp cornstarch or potato starch

NUTRITION

Calories 276 Kcal | fat 17 g | Carbohydrate 8 g | Protein 21 g

INSTRUCTIONS

1. To rehydrate dried shiitake mushrooms, place them in a medium dish with a little water and let them soak for a few minutes. The reconstituted mushrooms should be squeezed to remove any excess water.
2. Mushroom stems should be removed and chopped. Add all of the ingredients to a medium bowl and stir well.
3. With a back-of-the-knife mince, tenderize the ground pork. Add the meat and chopped mushrooms to the big bowl.
4. Slice green onions, add pork to the dish and stir to combine. For garnish, save some green onions.
5. Peel the ginger and coarsely chop or grate it if using fresh ginger. Pre-ground raw ginger may also be purchased in tubes. Add it to the meat mixture and stir well to combine.
6. Add salt, sesame oil, black pepper, sake, & soy sauce to the mixture. Add potato starch to a meat mixture and combine with your hands until fully combined.
7. Begin boiling water in the steamer. Lay down two or three patties, depending on how large the patties are and how many patties you have in your dish.
8. Cook for 10-15 minutes over high heat until the meat is tender and the juices are clear.
9. Use more sesame oil & sliced green onions to top the patties before serving.

DAIKON & CUCUMBER SUNOMONO SALAD

Preparation — **25 MIN**

Cook Time — **0 MIN**

Servings — **4**

INGREDIENTS

- 1 cucumber small, sliced crosswise thinly
- 1 daikon radish small piece
- 1 tsp salt
- 5 tbsp vinegar rice
- 2 tbsp sugar

NUTRITION

Calories 49 Kcal | fat 0 g | Carbohydrate 11 g | Protein 1 g

INSTRUCTIONS

1. Salt and pepper the cucumber & daikon pieces in a wide bowl. Sweating the veggies should take anywhere from five to ten minutes at most.
2. Drain both daikon & cucumber slices after washing and rinsing them well.
3. Gently drain out any extra liquid from the veggies and place them in a fresh dish.
4. Stir together the rice vinegar & sugar in a small separate bowl until thoroughly combined.
5. Over cucumber & daikon slices, pour your vinegar mixture. For around 15 minutes, let the flavors come together.
6. Scoop up a portion for each person and serve.
7. Alternatively, place the salad in the refrigerator for at least 30 minutes to allow it to cool.
8. Prepare the food and serve it to your guests.

KARASHI MENTAIKO & SPINACH SPAGHETTI

Preparation — **8 MIN**

Cook Time — **10 MIN**

Servings — **4**

INGREDIENTS

- 1 tsp oil olive
- 1 & ½ tsp butter unsalted
- ¼ cup yellow onion chopped
- ½ cup spinach baby
- 1-2 cups spaghetti cooked
- 1 oz cod roe (mentaiko, karashi mentaiko, or tarako)
- 1 white pepper dash
- 1 kizami nori sheet
- sliced Dried seaweed
- Shiso, sliced into chiffonade

INSTRUCTIONS

1. Cook pasta for 8 mins or unless al dente is in a pot of boiling water. Remove the drain and put it aside.
2. Remove the mentaiko sac's thin membrane & discard it. Eggs are the only thing you need to keep in mind.
3. Olive oil should be heated over medium-high heat in a big pan. Melt the butter before adding it to the mixture. Sauté the onion until transparent, then add it to the pan.
4. Turn down the heat to a simmer. Cook pasta according to package directions and toss with butter, olive oil, & onions in a large skillet over medium-high heat. The spinach should just be slightly wilted before adding it to the dish. Toss in a pinch of white pepper for flavor.
5. Take the pan off the heat. Ensure that the noodles are covered with cod roe before adding the raw mentaiko. Cod roe may be prepared to your liking by simply mixing it into the spaghetti and cooking it over moderate flame till the roe gets a delicate pink color.

NUTRITION

Calories 93 Kcal | fat 3 g |
Carbohydrate 12 g |
Protein 4 g

JAPANESE KURI KINTON

Preparation — **15 MIN**

Cook Time — **30 MIN**

Servings — **6**

INGREDIENTS

- 1 lb satsumaimo peeled sweet potatoes
- ¼ cup syrup Kuri-no-kanroni
- 8-12 chestnuts
- 1 & ½ cups of sugar
- 1 tbsp mirin
- 2 kuchinashi-no-mi dried

NUTRITION

Calories 344 Kcal | fat 0 g | Carbohydrate 85 g | Protein 2 g

INSTRUCTIONS

1. Spend around 15 minutes soaking the satsumaimo pieces in water before draining.
2. Pour sufficient water over satsumaimo to completely submerge them.
3. Crushed kuchinashi-no-mi may be added to the pot if it is wrapped in a piece of gauze. On high heat, bring to a rolling boil. Simmer over medium heat till the satsumaimo has softened.
4. Take off the kuchinashi-no-mi and rinse well.
5. Assemble the mixture by smashing it with your spatula through an open filter placed on the medium pan.
6. Using low heat, whisk in sugar to mashed satsumaimo. Stir in a quarter cup of syrup thoroughly. In addition, add mirin & boil until smooth. Remove from heat and stir in Kuri chestnuts. Serve the dish and enjoy!

STUFFED KELP ROLLS WITH SALMON

Preparation — **30 MIN**

Cook Time — **60 MIN**

Servings — **4**

INGREDIENTS

- 1 & ½-oz kelp dried kombu
- 4 cups of water
- 8 dried kanpyo strips
- salt pinch
- ¾-lb filet salmon
- ½ cup sauce soy
- 4 tbsp sugar
- 2 tbsp sake
- 4 tbsp mirin

NUTRITION

Calories 387 Kcal | fat 14 g |
Carbohydrate 31 g |
Protein 32 g

INSTRUCTIONS

1. Kombu (dry kelp) should be soaked for 10 minutes in water. This liquid may be saved for later use.
2. Rinse the dehydrated kanpyo strips after rubbing salt on them. Kanpyo should be soaked in water for around 15 minutes in a big dish.
3. Cut your salmon fillet into 5-inch-long strips as you do this. The salmon fillet should be placed over a sheet of malleable kombu, which should be rolled around it.
4. Strips of kanpyo should be used to tie your konbu roll closed. The rolls of kombu may be added to a medium saucepan.
5. Then, using water, which was used to rehydrate the kombu, add the conserved soaked liquid to the saucepan (dried kelp). Toss in the kombu rolls and enjoy! Cook over medium heat, occasionally stirring, until slightly thickened.
6. Reduce the temperature to a comfortable level. Add the sugars, sakes, mirin, and soy sauces to the saucepan.
7. Cook the kombu, salmon, & rolls in the simmering liquid for an hour on low heat until the fish is cooked through and the flavors of the liquid have been absorbed into the rolls.
8. Turn the temperature down. Allow the kelp rolls to cool in the saucepan before serving.
9. Place the kobumaki rolls on a chopping board after removing them from the saucepan. Divide each piece in half.

ENDOMAME KORROKE

Preparation — **15 MIN**

Cook Time — **30 MIN**

Servings — **4**

INGREDIENTS

- 250 g peas frozen
- ¼ tsp juice of the lemon
- 40 g butter
- 50 g finely chopped prawns raw
- sugar a pinch
- white pepper a pinch
- skewers bamboo
- 120 g blended breadcrumbs panko
- BATTER
- 100 g bread flour strong white
- ½ tsp powder baking
- 1 tbsp wine white
- 1 egg large, yolk & white separated
- ½ tbsp oil olive
- 200 ml milk whole

NUTRITION

Calories 494 Kcal | fat 25 g | Carbohydrate 48 g | Protein 17 g

INSTRUCTIONS

1. The peas should be blanched for one minute in hot water before being strained well. Boil the peas until tender, often turning, in a clean nonstick pan for 15 minutes. While the mixer is running, slowly drizzle lemon juice to get a smooth consistency.
2. Then, in a small skillet set over medium heat, gently sauté the butter & chopped prawns until the prawns become pink. Stir in the peas that have been pureed in a separate bowl. Sugar, pepper, and a bit of salt are needed. Cool fast by scraping into a mixing bowl and placing it over a larger bowl of ice.
3. Using a bamboo stick and a heaping tbsp (20g) mixture, form into an oval lollipop and refrigerate for one hour.
4. Flour & baking powder are combined in a bowl and then used to produce the batter. Whisk in wine, oil, egg yolk, and milk, then taste and adjust seasonings. Gently stir the egg whites into the flour mixture in a separate bowl until they form soft peaks.
5. The panko breadcrumbs should be placed in a shallow bowl and mixed well. Gently shake any excess batter out and sprinkle panko on the lollipops before placing them on a baking sheet.
6. Fill a third of the pan with oil & heat to 170 C or until a bread cube browns within 40 seconds. After 3 minutes of cooking, drain the skewers onto kitchen paper & serve.

CELERIAC KATSU SANDO

Preparation — **5 MIN**

Cook Time — **30 MIN**

Servings — **4**

INGREDIENTS

- 1 celeriac large
- olive oil, a drizzle
- 50 g well-seasoned flour plain
- 1 beaten egg
- 100 g breadcrumbs panko
- vegetable oil for frying

To serve

- 2 to 3 tbsp buttermilk
- 1 tbsp rice vinegar
- shredded celeriac off-cuts
- 8 slices of crust removed from white bread
- 4 tbsp sauce tonkatsu

INSTRUCTIONS

1. Line a roasting pan with baking paper & heat your oven to 170C/gas 5. Pour some olive oil over the slices of celeriac & season, then cover with Al foil. Cook for around 25 minutes in the oven, or until the meat is fork-tender. Allow enough time for cooling.
2. Salt, pepper, and panko breadcrumbs are all that are needed for this recipe. Before covering the celeriac in breadcrumbs, toss it in flour and shake off excess. Then dip it in a beaten egg and toss it one more.
3. Add more salt and pepper to the buttermilk, vinegar, & shredded celeriac to produce a fast remoulade.
4. Add your breaded celeriac pieces in batches to a big, deep frying pan and cook for 1 to 2 minutes from all sides or until they are crisp and golden. Drain over kitchen paper.
5. Assemble the celeriac steak & remoulade on top of the tonkatsu sauce on a large cutting board before adding the leftover bread pieces.

NUTRITION

Calories 423 Kcal | fat 14 g |
Carbohydrate 58 g |
Protein 12 g

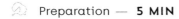

LITTLE GEM LETTUCE WITH TOSAZU

Preparation — **5 MIN**

Cook Time — **10 MIN**

Servings — **4**

INGREDIENTS

- 4 Little quartered Gem lettuces,
- 2 tbsp oil rapeseed
- sesame seeds toasted

Dressing

- 4 tbsp vinegar rice
- 1 tbsp sugar caster
- ½ tsp sauce soy
- 1 & ½ tsp mirin
- 2 g katsuobushi

INSTRUCTIONS

1. In a medium saucepan, combine the vinegar, soy sauce, mirin, sugar, and salt and bring to a simmer. Pour thru a sieve after katsuobushi has been added, if desired.
2. Season and toss the lettuce sections in rapeseed oil. A hot grill or griddle pan may be used to sear the lettuce cut-side down until it is properly browned on both sides.
3. Pour a few dressings over the pieces & sprinkle with the sesame seeds.

NUTRITION

Calories 183 Kcal | fat 6 g |
Carbohydrate 27 g |
Protein 3 g

KING PRAWN YAKI SOBA

Preparation — **10 MIN**

Cook Time — **20 MIN**

Servings — **2**

INGREDIENTS

- for frying oil
- 1 halved & sliced small onion
- 1 sliced green or red pepper
- 4 sliced spring onions
- 150 g butterflied king prawns raw
- bean sprouts, a handful
- 300 g ramen fresh or noodles egg
- pink shredded pickled ginger
- white & black sesame seeds

Yaki soba sauce

- 1 tsp sugar caster
- 1 tbsp sauce soy
- 1 tbsp sauce oyster
- ½ tbsp ketchup tomato
- 1 tbsp sauce Worcestershire
- ¼ tsp pepper white

NUTRITION

Calories 469 Kcal | fat 18 g | Carbohydrate 53 g | Protein 22 g

INSTRUCTIONS

1. Add the sauce ingredients and mix well.
2. In a frying pan, heat 2 tbsp of oil. Sauté for 3 to 4 minutes until onion & pepper are softened. Toss within spring onions & prawns, cook unless the prawns begin to turn pink and remove from heat.
3. Serve with a dollop of dipping sauce on top. Ginger & sesame seeds should be sprinkled on top of the dish.

QUICK JAPANESE-STYLE RICE SALAD

Preparation — **5 MIN**

Cook Time — **10 MIN**

Servings — **2**

INGREDIENTS

- 250 g basmati rice cooked
- 150 g king prawns cooked peeled
- ¼ diced cucumber
- 2 chopped spring onions
- 50 g defrosted edamame beans,
- 6 chopped radishes
- ½ diced avocado
- sesame seeds black to serve

Dressing

- 2 tbsp vinegar rice
- 1 tbsp sesame oil toasted
- 1 tbsp mirin
- 1 tbsp chopped pickled ginger

NUTRITION

Calories 415 Kcal | fat 18 g |
Carbohydrate 41 g |
Protein 20 g

INSTRUCTIONS

1. In a small dish, combine all of the dressing ingredients.
2. If you're using a pouch, cook the rice according to the directions on the bag before pouring it into a dish and breaking it up. Add half of the dressing and stir when heated.
3. When you've added the prawns and vegetables, mix them in again. Spoon the remaining dressing over the salad and serve immediately. Sprinkle sesame seeds on top of the finished dish if you'd like.

MARMITE CHICKEN

Preparation — **15 MIN**

Cook Time — **30 MIN**

Servings — **4**

INGREDIENTS

- 500 g chicken thighs boneless
- 1 crushed clove of garlic
- 1 tbsp sauce soy
- sunflower oil deep-frying
- 4 tbsp cornflour Japanese katakuriko
- Sweet cucumber & wakame pickle
- 160 ml vinegar rice
- 120 g sugar granulated
- 2 thinly sliced large cucumbers
- 2 tbsp salt sea
- 1 large thinly sliced red chili
- 2 tbsp wakame seaweed dried
- Marmite & soy sauce
- 2 tbsp Marmite
- 2 tbsp soy sauce dark
- 8 tbsp mirin
- 4 tbsp sake or rice wine Shaoxing

NUTRITION

Calories 402 Kcal | fat 16 g | Carbohydrate 27 g | Protein 32 g

INSTRUCTIONS

1. Add the sugar, vinegar, & 160ml of water to a saucepan and bring to a boil over medium heat. Remove from the heat and let it cool before storing it in an airtight container. Let it cool for an hour before serving. Using a colander, place the cucumber pieces in a bowl and sprinkle them liberally with salt. Cucumber slices should be covered with a heavy plate for an hour, after which time they should be drained of as much liquid as possible but not rinsed. Refrigerate the rice vinegar mixture, then add your cucumber & chili slices. Let them ferment for almost two hours.

2. Make bite-sized pieces of chicken and place them in a bowl with the garlic & soy sauce. Mix thoroughly and let sit for 30 minutes to 2 hours, if possible.

3. To prepare the dehydrated wakame seaweed for the pickles, soak it in ice water for 2 to 3 minutes, drain, press off the water, and cut any big pieces. Do this 20 minutes before serving your pickles. Mix in the wakame thoroughly with the pickle mixture. You may now serve the pickle, and any remains can be kept in the fridge for up to one month in an airtight container.

4. Then, combine the Marmite & soy sauce components in a separate dish and whisk until Marmite is completely dissolved.

5. The pan should be 1/3 full of sunflower oil and heated to 170C till a bread cube browns in 40 seconds. Chicken should be sprayed with cornflour or potato starch before adding to the pan. Drain the chicken on a dish lined using kitchen paper after cooking for 8 to 10 minutes or unless golden brown & cooked through.

6. In a skillet, boil up the Marmite & soy sauce unless the alcohol has evaporated, and then add chicken pieces, then stir well to cover them in it. Both spring onions & cucumber pickles should be served on the side as soon as possible.

ONIGIRAZU

Preparation — **10 MIN**

Cook Time — **35 MIN**

Servings — **2**

INGREDIENTS

- 150 g rice sushi
- 1 tbsp vinegar rice
- 4 nori sheets
- ½ shredded carrot
- 1 sliced avocado
- 150 g sliced tuna sashimi-grade
- 4 tbsp ginger pickled
- ¼ deseeded & sliced cucumber
- wasabi paste to serve
- soy sauce to serve

NUTRITION

Calories 517 Kcal | fat 16 g | Carbohydrate 62 g | Protein 28 g

INSTRUCTIONS

1. Take a look at the package's instructions and follow them exactly. Set aside to cool after being poured out onto a platter and sprinkled with rice vinegar & a little salt.

2. While you're waiting, place one nori sheet over the top of a layer of clingfilm over the work surface. Separate your rice into eight equal piles using damp hands, then press one of the piles into an 8-centimeter square in the center of the nori sheet. The nori sheet should be about one centimeter thick.

3. Layer on about a quarter of each of the following ingredients: carrot; avocado; tuna; ginger; cucumber Place a third rice square on the top. Use some water to bind the nori wrap over the rice, then wrap the sandwich in clingfilm and store in the fridge.

4. Chill until required, then repeat with the rest of your ingredients. To eat, split in half & serve with some wasabi & soy sauce as a dipping condiment.

SPINACH SALAD WITH SESAME DRESSING

V

Preparation — **10 MIN**

Cook Time — **5 MIN**

Servings — **4**

INGREDIENTS

- ½ lb of spinach
- 1 tsp salt kosher

Sesame Sauce

- 3 Tbsp sesame seeds white toasted
- 1 Tbsp sauce soy
- 1 Tbsp of sugar
- Sesame Sauce (for adults)
- 3 tbsp sesame seeds toasted white
- 1 & ½ Tbsp sauce soy
- 1 Tbsp of sugar
- ½ tsp of sake
- ½ tsp of mirin

NUTRITION

Calories 110 Kcal | fat 6 g | Carbohydrate 10 g | Protein 6 g

INSTRUCTIONS

SESAME SAUCE

1. To make the sesame sauce, lightly toast the sesame seeds inside a frying pan. Remove the skillet from the heat when two or three sesame seeds begin to burst out of it.
2. Using a pestle and mortar, pulverize the roasted sesame seeds. To add some interest, leave a few sesame seeds whole. Mix the sesame seeds and the ingredients for the sesame sauce.

SPINACH SALAD

3. Bring a big saucepan of lightly salted water to a boil. Once the water is boiling, add your spinach and simmer for 30 to 45 seconds, depending on how thick the spinach is. Tip: Unlike Japanese spinach, which must be cooked for at least one minute, American spinach is tender enough to consume raw.
4. Once you've removed your spinach from the water, please place it in an ice bath to halt any further cooking that may have occurred. The spinach may also be cooled by rinsing in cold water after being drained. Squeeze all water out of the spinach before storing it.
5. Put the spinach in a medium bowl and cut it into 1-2" (2.5-5 cm) before mixing it with the other ingredients.
6. Toss everything together with the sesame sauce. Cold or hot: Serve around room temperature or cooled.

CHICKEN KATSU CURRY

Preparation — **20 MIN**

Cook Time — **25 MIN**

Servings — **2**

INGREDIENTS

- seasoned flour for dusting
- 1 beaten egg
- 100 g breadcrumbs naturally dried
- 4 large chicken thighs, skinless, boneless
- 100 g rice basmati
- 75 g peas frozen
- soy sauce & sesame oil

Curry sauce

- 1 chopped onion
- 2 crushed cloves of garlic
- a small peeled & finely chopped chunk of ginger
- chili flakes a pinch
- oil for frying
- 1 tbsp flour plain or curry powder
- 350 ml stock chicken
- 1 tsp sugar brown

NUTRITION

Calories 816 Kcal | fat 21 g |
Carbohydrate 94 g |
Protein 58 g

INSTRUCTIONS

1. Set aside separate bowls for flour, egg, and breadcrumbs. Flour, egg, and breadcrumbs all go on top of the chicken before serving. Please put it in the fridge for 20 minutes, and then serve.

2. Soften the garlic, onion, and ginger for the curry sauce in a little oil. Make sure to whisk often to avoid clumps of flour & curry powder forming. For 15 minutes, add your chicken stock, then whisk in the sugar. Use a stick blender/food processor to mix the sauce to a creamy consistency.

3. Set the oven to 180°C. In a nonstick frying pan, heat 2 tbsp of oil. Once golden brown on all sides, remove the chicken to a baking sheet and bake for another 20 minutes, or until done.

4. Add the peas to the rice for the last two minutes of cooking. Drain well before adding a few sesames oil drops and soy sauce to the mixture. Serve the warmed sauce over the chicken & rice once sliced and placed on top.

MISO MACKEREL W/ CHILI BROWN RICE

Preparation — **5 MIN**

Cook Time — **15 MIN**

Servings — **2**

INGREDIENTS

- 2 mackerel whole
- oil
- 4 tbsp miso white
- 2 tsp caster sugar golden
- 2 tsp mirin
- 150 g brown rice
- 1 cm grated piece of ginger
- 1 seeded & finely chopped red chili
- 2 finely chopped spring onions

NUTRITION

Calories 612 Kcal | fat 23 g | Carbohydrate 75 g | Protein 24 g

INSTRUCTIONS

1. Cut all fillets from the fish and remove any visible tiny bones using the entire fish. Lay the skin-side down fillets on a tray with the oil. Brush the flesh of the fish with a combination of miso, sugar, and mirin. While the rice is cooking, marinate the meat.
2. Brown rice should be prepared. Stir together the ginger, chili, & spring onion inside a small bowl with a few drops of oil to taste. When the rice is finished cooking, transfer it to a bowl, add the ginger mix, & season generously with salt and pepper.
3. For approximately 5 minutes on each side, or unless the top is well browned and the fish is cooked through, preheat the grill to high. Serve the rice with the appetizers.

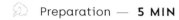

TSUKUNE & JAPANESE-STYLE QUINOA

Preparation — **10 MIN**

Cook Time — **30 MIN**

Servings — **4**

INGREDIENTS

- 450 g minced chicken
- 1 crushed clove of garlic
- 2 finely chopped spring onions
- 2 tsp ginger grated
- 4 tbsp breadcrumbs panko
- oil for frying
- 200 g red & black quinoa mixed
- a small, chopped bunch of coriander
- sesame oil to serve
- 5 tbsp mirin
- 4 tbsp sauce soy
- 1 juiced lemon
- 2 tbsp honey

NUTRITION

Calories 424 Kcal | fat 7 g |
Carbohydrate 56 g |
Protein 35 g

INSTRUCTIONS

1. Make your glaze by combining all of the ingredients in a small saucepan, then scoop off some glaze & put it aside for the quinoa. You may use your hands to combine everything in a dish of minced meat. Using approximately 2 tbsp of ingredients per meatball, form the meatballs and place them on a baking sheet. Three skewers per stick are recommended.

2. Tsukune may be fried in batches in a big, nonstick frying pan, ensuring they're browned on all sides and cooked thoroughly. Every time you flip them in the pan, brush them using the glaze.

3. Meantime, rinse your quinoa with cold water, stir it about with a whisk, and soak it for a few minutes before draining and drying. Reserving 4 tbsp of the cooking liquid is simple. Continue stirring till the grains are dry and beginning to brown & pop in a big frying pan or wok. The grains should be added to a skillet, covered with water, brought to a simmer, and then drained. In the frying pan, brown & smell nutty of the uncooked Four tbsp of grains.

4. Tip the quinoa onto each dish with the remaining glaze & coriander, tossing to coat.

5. To serve, arrange a few skewers on each dish and top with the toasted quinoa.

CORN DOGS

Preparation — **15 MIN**

Cook Time — **15 MIN**

Servings — **4**

INGREDIENTS

- 5.3 oz Hotcake Mix Japanese
- ½ cup milk whole
- 1 egg large
- 4 sausages/hot dogs
- 3 cups oil neutral-flavored
- For Serving
- mustard
- ketchup

INSTRUCTIONS

1. Cut every hot dog into half, based on the scale of the sausage.
2. Insert one chopstick or one lollipop stick at the end of every hot dog to hold it in place.
3. Mix the egg and milk in a big bowl.
4. Whisk in the hotcake mix until smooth.
5. Fill 3 to 4" of oil into a big Dutch oven, heavy pot, and deep fryer. Heat the oil to 320-340°F on a deep-frying thermometer on medium-high heat.
6. Fill a large glass halfway with the batter. Turn each hot dog to cover it well with the batter before dipping it in. Ensure your hot dog is covered evenly by allowing any extra batter to fall off it.
7. The hot dog should be lowered into the warm oil. Repeat the same with the second hot dog right away. Cook for approximately 3 minutes, or until golden brown. Corn dogs should be rotated to provide equal coloring.
8. Place on a wire rack or a tray coated with paper towels. Repeat with the leftover hot dogs & batter in two-dozen-strong batches. Serve your corn dogs with ketchup & mustard as soon as they're done cooking.

NUTRITION

Calories 346 Kcal | fat 25 g |
Carbohydrate 21 g |
Protein 10 g

LOTUS ROOT CHIPS

Preparation — **10 MIN**

Cook Time — **15 MIN**

Servings — **2**

INGREDIENTS

- 1 root lotus
- 2 cups of water (lotus root for soaking)
- 1 tsp vinegar rice
- 1 cup oil neutral-flavored

For Seasoning

- pink salt Himalayan
- aonori (green laver dried seaweed)

INSTRUCTIONS

1. Thoroughly wash the lotus root. Slice your lotus root into 1/8-inch-thick slices using a mandolin slicer.
2. Stir together water & rice vinegar in a dish and serve. For 5 to 10 minutes, soak your lotus root pieces in vinegared water. Adding vinegar to the water will keep lotus roots from discoloring and turn them white.
3. Make sure to thoroughly rinse and drain all ingredients before using them.
4. Make careful to pat dry with a paper towel to remove all the water.
5. Add the oil to medium-high heat and bring it to 340 degrees Fahrenheit. To test whether the lotus root is ready, just drop a piece of it. You may deep fry it if it rises immediately away.
6. Lotus root slices should be deep-fried until crispy & golden.
7. Spread them out on a wire rack to absorb excess oil once they've been perfectly cooked. Wait until you're ready to eat before adding salt & aonori to your food.

NUTRITION

Calories 205 Kcal | fat 14 g |
Carbohydrate 20 g |
Protein 3 g

SESAME WARM MUSHROOM SALAD

Preparation — **15 MIN**

Cook Time — **15 MIN**

Servings — **4**

INGREDIENTS

- 9.5 oz mushrooms king oyster
- 5 mushrooms shiitake
- 7 oz mushrooms enoki
- 3.5 oz mushrooms shimeji
- 1 mizuna bunch
- 1 & ½ Tbsp oil neutral-flavored
- ½ tsp sea salt or kosher
- 1 tbsp of sake
- 1 tsp sesame oil roasted

Sesame Dressing:

- 3 tbsp sesame seeds toasted white
- 3 Tbsp unseasoned rice vinegar
- 2 Tbsp sauce soy
- 1 Tbsp of mirin
- 1 Tbsp of sugar

NUTRITION

Calories 157 Kcal | fat 9 g |
Carbohydrate 15 g |
Protein 6 g

INSTRUCTIONS

TO MAKE THE DRESSING:

1. Toasted sesame seeds should be toasted for 3-5 minutes in a dry frying pan. Toasting might be uneven if the skillet isn't stirred and shaken often enough. Place the roasted sesame seeds in the pestle and mortar of your choice. Halfway grind your sesame seeds. With no mortar and pestle in your kitchen, you may grind with your hands or put it in the food processor.

2. Toasted sesame seeds go into the mixture of mirin, sugar, rice vinegar, and soy sauce.

TO CUT INGREDIENTS:

3. Cut king oyster mushrooms in half lengthwise, approximately 5 centimeters.

4. Make slivers of it by chopping it up. Slice the shiitake mushrooms into thin strips and discard the stems.

5. Separate the enoki mushrooms by slicing off their stems. Separate shimeji mushrooms by slicing off the base.

6. The end of the mizuna should be discarded, and the mizuna should be cut into 5 cm length pieces.

TO COOK INGREDIENTS:

7. A big frying pan with medium heat and oil is ideal for this. Add all of the mushrooms to the pot and mix well.

8. Add the kosher salt to the mushrooms and cook until tender. After that, cook the sake for 2 minutes with a lid on over medium heat.

9. Toss the salad with the sesame dressing. Pour sesame oil over the ingredients and combine well.

10. Add the mizuna just before turning off the heat and quickly stir everything together. As long as there is heat in the pan, the mizuna will continue cooking. Serve hot from a serving dish.

ASIAN COLESLAW WITH SESAME DRESSING

Preparation — **20 MIN**

Cook Time — **0 MIN**

Servings — **4**

INGREDIENTS

- 1 cabbage
- 1 bunch of cilantros
- 1 green scallion/onion
- 1 carrot
- other choices vegetable

Dressing

- ½ cup vinegar apple cider
- 3 Tbsp of sugar
- 3 Tbsp sesame oil roasted
- 2 Tbsp white toasted sesame seeds
- ¼ tsp of sea salt or kosher
- black pepper freshly ground

INSTRUCTIONS

1. If required, cut the length of the carrot in half & julienne it.
2. Cut the cilantro into 12-inch sections and the green onions into very small slices.
3. Cut your cabbage into small strips after removing the core.
4. When using two types of cabbage, be sure to trim the second one. Drain well after washing in cold water.
5. Add all of the veggies to the dressing within the bowl. Refrigerate for at least 30 mins before serving after tossing everything together.

NUTRITION

Calories 161 Kcal | fat 8 g |
Carbohydrate 22 g |
Protein 4 g

JAPANESE CUCUMBER SALAD

Preparation — **15 MIN**

Cook Time — **0 MIN**

Servings — **4**

INGREDIENTS

- 2 Persian cucumbers or Japanese
- ½ tsp sea salt or kosher
- 1 Tbsp wakame seaweed dried
- ½ Tbsp sesame seeds toasted white

Seasoning

- 4 Tbsp unseasoned rice vinegar
- 2 Tbsp of sugar
- ½ tsp sea salt or kosher
- ½ tsp soy sauce
- To Make Variations (each ingredient is added to the recipe above)
- 4 crab meat pieces imitation
- 2 oz sashimi octopus
- 2 Tbsp of shirasu

INSTRUCTIONS

1. Add rice vinegar, sugar, kosher salt, and soy sauce to a medium bowl. Mix thoroughly. You may temper the vinegar flavor with a very little quantity of dashi if it is too overpowering.

MAKE SUNOMONO

2. Allow 10 minutes of rehydration time for 1 tbsp of dried wakame seaweed.
3. To make striped cucumbers, peel your cucumbers in alternating directions. After that, cut them into rounds by slicing them very thinly.
4. Mix in 12 tsp of kosher salt and mash them together gently. Wait for five minutes before continuing. Soluble cucumber juice may be drawn out by adding salt.
5. Wakame seaweed & cucumber should be squeezed for their water. Toss them all together in the dish with the spices.

NUTRITION

Calories 39 Kcal | fat 1 g | Carbohydrate 5 g | Protein 3 g

GREEN BEAN GOMAAE

Preparation — **10 MIN**

Cook Time — **10 MIN**

Servings — **4**

INGREDIENTS

- ½ lb beans green
- 1 tsp sea salt or kosher

The Dressing

- 3 tbsp sesame seeds toasted white
- 1 Tbsp sauce soy
- 1 Tbsp of sugar

INSTRUCTIONS

1. BRING WATER TO BOIL IN the POT! To toast the sesame seeds, gently shake the pan for two minutes in a non-greased pan, even if they've already been toasted. Make sure not to overheat.

2. Make the sauce by grinding the sesame seeds using a pestle and mortar but leave a few sesame seeds whole for texture. Mix in the soy sauce & sugar. The dressing is rather a thick paste. Set away for later.

3. The green beans need to be cooked to remove any potential threat from your green beans that have not been clipped, break the tip of one end with your fingers and drag it down the bean. Pull the second end of the bean in the same direction as the first one.

4. Bring a pot of water to a boil, then add the green beans and a pinch of salt. If you want to keep the green beans crisp and brilliant green yet tender, cook them for about 4 minutes.

5. Remove them from the fire, set them in the filter, and rapidly rinse them under cold water to prevent them from cooking. To keep green beans from turning brown, shock them with cold water. No need to refrigerate; the beans should remain warm. Then, using a sharp knife, cut them into 2-inch-long pieces after thoroughly drying them off with a clean towel.

6. Pour the sesame dressing over the heated beans and toss to combine. Serve at ambient temperature or cooled if preferred.

NUTRITION

Calories 66 Kcal | fat 3 g |
Carbohydrate 9 g |
Protein 3 g

SPINACH WITH SESAME MISO SAUCE

Preparation — **10 MIN**

Cook Time — **5 MIN**

Servings — **4**

INGREDIENTS

- ¼ tsp sea salt or kosher
- 6 oz of spinach
- Sesame Miso Sauce
- 2 Tbsp of mirin
- 3 Tbsp sesame seeds white toasted
- 3 tsp of miso
- 2 tsp of sugar
- 1 tsp of soy sauce

NUTRITION

Calories 52 Kcal | fat 2 g | Carbohydrate 5 g | Protein 2 g

INSTRUCTIONS

1. Make a list of everything you need. Add water to a large saucepan and bring it to a boil. [Optional] Using a frying pan, toast sesame seeds on low heat if they are not already toasted or roasted to your liking. Remove the skillet from the heat when two or three sesame seeds begin to burst out of it.
2. Stir in 1 tbsp. Mirin to a small pot of simmering water while you wait. Cook for 30 seconds at medium heat unless the alcohol has evaporated. Set away for later.
3. 2 Tbsp sesame seeds should be pounded in a surikogi (pestle) in the mortar of a Suribachi (mortar). The texture is always a good thing.
4. Miso paste, sugar, alcohol-free mirin, and soy sauce should be added and mixed well.
5. Salt should be added to the boiling water. The stems of the spinach leaves should be held so that you can begin blanching them from the top down. Take a look at it in 15 seconds. 30 seconds after letting go of the green section, continue cooking
6. To stop the spinach from cooking, remove it from the water and submerge it in cold water. Drain the spinach and run it under cold water to chill it down.
7. Squeeze the water out of the spinach before storing it.
8. Add the spinach to the bowl by slicing it into 2" (5cm) pieces.
9. Toss the spinach in with the sauce. Serve at ambient temperature or cooled if preferred.

HIJIKI SEAWEED SALAD

Preparation — **15 MIN**

Cook Time — **45 MIN**

Servings — **4**

INGREDIENTS

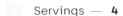

- ½ cup hijiki seaweed dried
- 4 cups for soaking water
- 2 aburaage
- 4 oz konnyaku
- 3 oz of carrot
- ¼ root lotus
- 1 Tbsp oil neutral-flavored
- 1/3 cup edamame shelled
- 2 dashi cups
- Seasonings:
- ¼ cup of mirin
- 2 Tbsp of sugar
- ¼ cup sauce soy

INSTRUCTIONS

1. For 30 minutes, soak dry hijiki in 4 water cups.
2. Drizzle water over a big fine sieve and rinse thoroughly.
3. Pour boiling water over the aburaage in a small saucepan. Removing the aburaage of the extra oil will be a breeze with this method. Make thin slices by slicing the meat in half lengthwise.
4. Remove the scent of konnyaku by boiling it in water for 3 minutes. It also enhances the texture of the konnyaku by increasing the absorption of tastes.
5. Prepare the carrots by julienne slicing them.
6. Thinly slice the lotus root
7. In a medium saucepan, heat the oil over medium heat. Cook the carrots and lotus root in the oil until they are well-coated.
8. It's time to put in the hijiki and then the konnyaku. Make a concoction.
9. Add some dashi and bring to a boil.
10. Take care to thoroughly incorporate all of the spices. Cook for around 20-30 minutes with the lid on medium heat.
11. Add in the edamame.
12. Cook your sauce unless you can see the base of the pan uncovered for the remainder of the cooking time.

NUTRITION

Calories 128 Kcal | fat 3 g |
Carbohydrate 17 g |
Protein 5 g

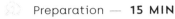

CHRYSANTHEMUM GREENS & TOFU SALAD

Preparation — **10 MIN**

Cook Time — **33 MIN**

Servings — **6**

INGREDIENTS

- ½ lb of shungiku
- 7 oz tofu medium-firm
- Seasonings
- 4 tbsp sesame seeds toasted white
- 1 Tbsp of sugar
- 3 tsp miso
- 2 tsp mirin
- 2 tsp soy sauce
- ¼ tsp sea salt or kosher

NUTRITION

Calories 85 Kcal | fat 4 g |
Carbohydrate 6 g |
Protein 5 g

INSTRUCTIONS

1. Make a list of everything you need. To preserve any remaining tofu, place it in the airtight container & fill it with water to the brim. Use it in the next few days after putting it in the fridge.

TO PREPARE TOFU

2. Make sure you don't miss this step. Tofu should not be drained entirely, but a little water should be removed to prevent the dressing from becoming overly wet. Paper towels are used to wrap the tofu. Place the tofu in its wrapper on a dish or tray. Drain the tofu by placing another tray or dish on top and placing a heavy item on top. Put on a timer for around 20-30 minutes. Tofu wrapped in paper may also be microwaved for one minute (1200W).

TO PREPARE SESAME SEEDS

3. Toasted sesame seeds should be aromatic and start to burst when toasted in the frying pan with regular stirring.

4. Grinder pounding the sesame seeds in the Japanese mortar.

TO PREPARE CHRYSANTHEMUM GREENS

5. Chrysanthemum leaves' tips should be clipped and thrown away. After that, cut them into 5-centimeter (2-inch) pieces. Maintain a clear separation between the stems and leaves.

6. Add water to a large saucepan and bring it to a boil. Begin the cooking process by boiling the stems for around 15 seconds.

7. Cook for another 5 seconds before adding the stems and leaves.

8. After that, add your leafy greens and cook for around 5 seconds under the water.

9. Drain all leaves & shock your greens in cold water as rapidly as possible. Leaves will become brilliant green due to this procedure, preventing them from overcooking. Squeeze out the water and store it in an airtight container.

TO MAKE TOFU DRESSING

10. Remove the tofu's weight and then the paper towel wrapper.

11. In a mortar, combine the sesame seeds and tofu. Once the tofu has been mashed and ground with the pestle, it is ready to be served.

12. Mix the tofu with the miso, soy sauce, sugar, mirin, & salt until well-combined. Add salt to taste to the tofu mixture at this point. Because the greens will dilute the taste, you'll want it to be a little saltier than you normally would.

TO ASSEMBLE

13. Add these greens to a tofu mixture and stir well to incorporate them into the dish. It's up to you whether or not you want to refrigerate the mixture for around 30 minutes before serving.

SPICY JAPANESE PICKLED CUCUMBERS

Preparation — **15 MIN**

Cook Time — **0 MIN**

Servings — **3**

INGREDIENTS

- 2 Persian cucumbers or Japanese
- ½ tsp sea salt or kosher
- ½ tsp sesame seeds toasted white

For Seasonings

- 2 Tbsp sauce soy
- 2 Tbsp sesame oil roasted
- ½ tsp of la-yu
- ½ tsp of sugar

NUTRITION

Calories 37 Kcal | fat 3 g |
Carbohydrate 2 g |
Protein 1 g

INSTRUCTIONS

1. Combine all the ingredients in a small bowl and stir well to make the spices.
2. Cut off a 1-inch [1.3 cm] broad slice of cucumber lengthwise but keep a strip of skin attached. Cucumber slices that have been prepared in this manner will have a darker green hue to them & an added crunch.
3. Rangiri is a Japanese method for slicing cucumbers.
4. Rub the cucumbers with your hands after sprinkling them with salt. This is a crucial stage in the process of pickling cucumbers.
5. Transfer to the sieve after 5 minutes on the chopping board. Rinse your salt underneath running water as quickly as possible.
6. Pat the cucumber dry with a paper towel.
7. Add the spices to a container. Add the cucumber and mix well.
8. The container or bag should be closed or sealed once the air has been pushed out. Rub your cucumber from the outside of the bag or shake the container.
9. Because of the weight, you may place it immediately on top of your cucumber to preserve it. The weight of the jar will speed up the process of pickling. Refrigerate for at least six hours, preferably overnight.

JAPANESE OKRA SALAD

Preparation — **10 MIN**

Cook Time — **5 MIN**

Servings — **3**

INGREDIENTS

- 10 okras
- ½ tsp sea salt or kosher

Marinade

- 2 cups of dashi
- 3 Tbsp of usukuchi
- 3 Tbsp of mirin

INSTRUCTIONS

1. Remove the okra's tail. Remove the tough outer layer of the okra's stem, as indicated in the illustration below.
2. They should resemble this. Water will seep in if you leave the end uncut.
3. Boil a sufficient amount of water. Gently massage the okras with kosher salt on a chopping board. Cucumbers, for example, brightened up, and their bitterness was eliminated with this simple trick.
4. Okras should be blanched in boiling water for around 1-2 minutes after the water has risen to a boil.
5. Cool your okras in cold water after draining. Once they've cooled, take them from the water and gently squeeze them to remove any extra moisture. Set away for later.
6. Add mirin to a small pot and allow the alcohol to evaporate for a few seconds.
7. Dashi & soy sauce should be added after the alcohol odor has faded. Once it has reached a rolling boil, remove it from the heat and put it aside.
8. Bake the okras in a glass baking dish at least 3 inches deep. Put in the marinade while it's still heated and serve the meal. Before serving, let the tea steep for 1-2 hours.

NUTRITION

Calories 19 Kcal | fat 1 g |
Carbohydrate 3 g |
Protein 1 g

JAPANESE PICKLED CABBAGE

Preparation — **5 MIN**

Cook Time — **15 MIN**

Servings — **4**

INGREDIENTS

- ½ cabbage head
- ½ Persian cucumber or Japanese
- 1 chili pepper dried red
- 1-piece dried kombu
- 1 & ¼ tsp sea salt or kosher

Toppings (optional)

- sesame seeds toasted white
- sauce soy

INSTRUCTIONS

1. Cut the cabbage into 1-2" pieces and discard the core.
2. Peel and halve the cucumber. Once this is done, slice it thinly across the grain.
3. Round out the red chili by removing the seeds and slicing them. Avoid touching the seeds with bare hands or fingers while managing them.
4. To make kombu simpler to cut into thin strips, cook it over an open flame until it is soft.
5. Add kosher salt to the sealed plastic bag with the rest of the contents.
6. Rub the cabbage with your hands until it is pliable. Close your plastic bag securely after removing all of the air in it.
7. To pickle the bag, lay it beneath a heavy item and let it sit for 2-3 hours in a cold or refrigerated area.
8. Remove the cabbage from the brine and squeeze off the remaining liquid.

NUTRITION

Calories 31 Kcal | fat 1 g |
Carbohydrate 7 g |
Protein 2 g

SIMMERED FRIED TOFU AND GREENS

Preparation — **10 MIN**

Cook Time — **10 MIN**

Servings — **4**

INGREDIENTS

- 1 aburaage piece
- 6 oz of komatsuna
- 2 cups of dashi
- ½ tsp of sauce soy
- ½ tsp sea salt or kosher

NUTRITION

Calories 28 Kcal | fat 1 g |
Carbohydrate 5 g |
Protein 2 g

INSTRUCTIONS

1. To prepare your greens, trim the bottoms off and slice them into 2-inch (5-centimeter) pieces.
2. 3/8-inch-thick aburaage should be cut into pieces (1 cm).
3. Bring dashi & aburaage to a simmer in a small saucepan. Soy sauce & salt may be added after reaching a simmering point.
4. Add the greens' dense sections (stems) after mixing everything. Add the greens' delicate sections (leaves) after mixing everything and cooking for 1-2 minutes.
5. Simmer for 3 minutes on low heat after combining. Steep the meal in an airtight container by allowing it to cool down.

PICKLED DAIKON

Preparation — **10 MIN**

Cook Time — **0 MIN**

Servings — **4**

INGREDIENTS

- 1 lb radish daikon
- 1 chili pepper dried red
- 2 Tbsp rice vinegar
- 1 tsp of sake
- 1 Tbsp Sea salt or kosher
- 1/3 cup of sugar

INSTRUCTIONS

1. Slice the daikon into 14-inch (6 mm) slices after peeling it.
2. If you want your food less hot, chop the chili peppers into little pieces and remove their seeds.
3. In a Ziploc bag, combine all of the ingredients and massage well.
4. Close the bag after removing all of the air. During the first 2-3 hours, you'll begin to like it.

Calories 34 Kcal | fat 1 g | Carbohydrate 8 g | Protein 1 g

JAPANESE LOTUS ROOT STIR-FRY

Preparation — **15 MIN**

Cook Time — **15 MIN**

Servings — **4**

INGREDIENTS

- 8 oz root lotus
- 1 cup of water
- 1 tsp vinegar rice
- 1 chili pepper dried red
- 1 Tbsp sesame oil roasted
- ½ Tbsp sesame seeds toasted white

Seasonings

- 2 Tbsp sake
- 2 Tbsp mirin
- 1 Tbsp sugar
- 2 Tbsp sauce soy

INSTRUCTIONS

1. Make two halves using the lotus root after peeling it.
2. The lotus root should be sliced very thinly. Add rice vinegar & water to a bowl and mix well.
3. Soak the lotus root slices in vinegar water for 3 to 5 minutes to avoid discoloration.
4. Remove the seeds from the red chili pepper by cutting off the tip, then slicing the pepper into rounds. Keep the seeds in the dish if you want it hot.
5. The sesame oil should be heated to medium heat in a big frying pan, and the lotus root should be added and stir-fried.
6. Add the sake, mirin, & sugar when the lotus root becomes transparent. Let the booze dry up.
7. Be sure to blend the red chili powder with the soy sauce before adding it. Soy sauce is added at the end since it may easily burn.
8. Toss in the sesame seeds after the liquid has evaporated. Serve at room temperature, warm or cool. Keep in an airtight jar in the fridge for three or four days.

NUTRITION

Calories 102 Kcal | Fat 4 g | Carbohydrate 13 g | Protein 2 g

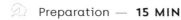

SIMMERED KIRIBOSHI DAIKON

Preparation — **10 MIN**

Cook Time — **30 MIN**

Servings — **4**

INGREDIENTS

- 1.4 oz dried kiriboshi daikon
- 1-piece deep-fried aburaage
- ⊠-½ carrot
- 1 Tbsp oil neutral-flavored

Seasonings

- 1 cup of dashi
- ½ cup of reserved water
- 2 Tbsp sake
- 3 Tbsp mirin
- 4 tsp sugar
- ¼ tsp sea salt or kosher
- 2 Tbsp sauce soy

INSTRUCTIONS

1. Rinse the kiriboshi daikon quickly and soak it in water for 15 to 20 minutes.
2. Take out ½ cup of the soaking water and save it aside for later. Drain and press the water out. 1–2-inch slices are best.
3. To remove excess oil, bring a pot of water to a boil & blanch the aburage for 30 seconds. Thinly slicing the meat
4. Cut the carrot into julienne strips after peeling it.
5. In a large saucepan, bring the oil to a boil over medium-high heat. Toss the Kiriboshi Daikon with the carrots and aburaage and coat them in oil for a few minutes before serving
6. 2 tbsp sake, 2 tbsp mirin, 2 tbsp sugar, 18 tsp kosher salt and 1 cup dashi to a boil.
7. Add 2 Tbsp of soy sauce to the boiling water.
8. Put an otoshibuta (drop cover) on & cook on medium heat for 15-20 minutes until the liquid is practically gone.

NUTRITION

Calories 111 Kcal | fat 4 g |
Carbohydrate 14 g |
Protein 3 g

SPICY BEAN SPROUT SALAD

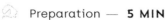

Preparation — **5 MIN**

Cook Time — **1 MIN**

Servings — **4**

INGREDIENTS

- 12 oz sprouts bean
- 1 tbsp sesame seeds toasted
- green scallion/onion

Seasonings

- 2 Tbsp sesame oil roasted
- 1 & ½ tsp sauce soy
- 1 & ½ tsp togarashi shichimi
- ½ tsp sea salt or kosher
- black pepper freshly ground

INSTRUCTIONS

1. Cook the bean sprouts in a big saucepan of salted water for 1 to 2 minutes.
2. The water should be drained completely after cooking.
3. In a medium bowl, combine all of the spices.
4. Mix in the fried bean sprouts until everything is well-combined. Sesame seeds may be sprinkled on the dish. If desired, top with scallion.

NUTRITION

Calories 85 Kcal | fat 6 g | Carbohydrate 6 g | Protein 3 g

SPICY TUNA DONBURI RICE BOWL

Preparation — **15 MIN**

Cook Time — **0 MIN**

Servings — **2**

INGREDIENTS

- 4 cups Japanese rice cooked
- 1/2-pound tuna, diced
- 2 tbsp Japanese mayonnaise
- 1 tbsp sauce Sriracha
- ¼ tsp oil sesame
- 1/8 tsp shichimi togarashi
- 6 tbsp oil chili

INSTRUCTIONS

1. Donburi-style bowls, bigger than typical rice bowls, are ideal for serving rice. Check the temperature of the rice before proceeding.
2. Crush the tuna into a fine paste. Squeeze out as much air as possible from the minced tuna before adding it to a medium-sized dish with Japanese mayo, Sriracha sauce, shichimi togarashi, & Rayu chili oil.
3. Spread the mixture liberally over the rice into donburi bowls after dividing it in half. Sprinkle sesame seeds, green onions, & soy sauce over top of each spicy tuna donburi.

Calories 1119 Kcal | fat 52 g | Carbohydrate 120 g | Protein 38 g

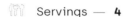

JAPANESE BURDOCK ROOT SALAD

Preparation — **20 MIN**

Cook Time — **10 MIN**

Servings — **3**

INGREDIENTS

- 1 burdock root gobo
- 1.5-inch carrot
- 1 Tbsp unseasoned rice vinegar
- ½ tsp sauce soy
- 1 tsp sesame oil roasted
- 1 & ½ tsp of sugar
- 4 tbsp sesame seeds toasted white
- 3 to 4 Tbsp mayonnaise Japanese
- togarashi shichimi (seven spice Japanese)

INSTRUCTIONS

1. Get rid of any filth on the gobo by washing it. Remove the skin by scraping it off with the knife's back. Slice diagonally into 1/8-inch-thick pieces.
2. Remove bitterness & oxidation by cutting gobo into 1/8-inch-thick sticks and soaking them in water.
3. Make gobo-sized sticks out of the carrot by slicing it in half.
4. Cook grated carrot for one minute in 2 cups of boiling water. The carrot may be scooped up with a sieve or a slotted spoon.
5. Pour in the drained gobo and simmer for a further two minutes.
6. Toss in a large bowl and drain well.
7. Make sure to add the vinegar, soy sauce, and sesame oil while the gobo is still hot.
8. A tsp of sugar is all that is needed. This aids in the absorption of spices via gobo. Before adding mayonnaise, let them cool down.
9. With a mortar and pestle, grind 3 tbsp of sesame seeds.
10. Add the grated carrot, 3-4 tbsp of Japanese mayonnaise, and the sesame seeds to the dressing and mix well. Add Shichimi Togarashi over the top if you want your food hot.

NUTRITION

Calories 205 Kcal | fat 16 g |
Carbohydrate 14 g |
Protein 3 g

JAPANESE POTATO SALAD

Preparation — **20 MIN**

Cook Time — **30 MIN**

Servings — **6**

INGREDIENTS

- 2 potatoes russet
- 2 tsp sea salt or kosher
- ¼ cup canned corn or frozen
- 1 egg large
- 1 cucumber Persian
- 2 oz of carrot
- 1 tsp sea salt or kosher
- 2 slices of Forest ham Black

For the Seasonings

- 1 Tbsp vinegar rice
- black pepper freshly ground
- 6 Tbsp mayonnaise Japanese

NUTRITION

Calories 198 Kcal | fat 12 g | Carbohydrate 19 g | Protein 5 g

INSTRUCTIONS

1. Using a knife, cut the potatoes into 112-inch (3.8-cm) pieces. For uniform cooking, they should be around the same size.
2. Pour 1 inch of cold water over the potatoes inside a medium saucepan and bring the water to a boil (2.5 cm). In a saucepan over medium-high heat, add salt to cook the potatoes. Avoid a boil-over by covering the lid but keeping it slightly ajar. To ensure that the potatoes cook evenly, begin cooking them in chilly water.
3. Add salt and pepper to taste, then turn the heat down to medium-low when the water has boiled. Cook for 15 minutes at a slow boil or until a spear easily passes through a potato.
4. Leave a little opening on one side of the cover and drain the pot of water entirely. Add the potatoes back to the saucepan and return it to the burner on medium heat, stirring the pot regularly to prevent the potatoes from sticking. Remove the saucepan from the heat as soon as there is no more liquid.
5. Lightly mash the potatoes, reserving some tiny pieces for a more authentic appearance. Add potatoes to the large bowl and mix well.
6. Salt & pepper should be added to the potatoes while still cooking. Set aside for a few minutes to cool off.

TO PREPARE THE OTHER INGREDIENTS

7. You may begin prepping the other ingredients while you boil the potatoes. Put some water on the stove and bring the frozen corn to a boil.

8. Set aside the cooled corn in the fine-mesh strainer. Boil an egg in medium water in the same pot, starting from cold. Boil for 11-12 minutes, then decrease the heat to a simmer and set a timer for that amount of time.

9. When a timer beeps, remove the shell and chill the egg under cold water.

10. Cut the egg into smaller pieces by slicing it in half. Set aside for a few minutes to cool off.

11. Thinly slice the cucumber (leave part of the peel on to create stripes). Before slicing, you might have to cut the cucumber in half or quadruple lengthwise.

12. To get thin slices, slice the carrot lengthwise in half or quarters. Use a mandoline slicing tool if you need assistance.

13. Salting in the following step may not work if your slices are too thick. Instead, you may microwave them in a water-filled microwave-safe container. To avoid mushy carrots, heat them in the microwave for several seconds until a spear can easily penetrate them. Let the water cool before draining it. If you choose this route, you can avoid the salting step later.

14. To prepare the cucumbers, massage them in your hands with half of the salt (for the cucumbers and carrots) and let them stand for approximately five minutes to release their moisture.

15. Beads of liquid will begin to appear on the surface of cucumbers. Salt acts as a scavenger, sucking moisture from the veggies through osmosis. There is a risk of water escaping from the veggies and reducing the taste of the salad.

16. Allow the carrots to rest for 5-7 minutes after sprinkling them with the second half of the salt and kneading them with your hands.

17. Quickly rinse beneath running water to remove the salt from cucumber & carrot slices inside a filter. Remove any excess moisture from the cucumber & carrot slices by squeezing them.

18. Make 1-inch (2.5 cm) wide strips of the ham and put them aside.

TO ASSEMBLE

19. Combine all ingredients in a large bowl and stir well. Incorporate around two-thirds of Japanese mayonnaise.

20. Consider adding additional mayonnaise after tasting it. The last third of mayonnaise was applied. Before serving, chill the potato salad in the refrigerator for 30-60 minutes.

STEAMED CAKE

Preparation — **10 MIN**

Cook Time — **10 MIN**

Servings — **4**

INGREDIENTS

- For Basic Steamed Cake
- ½ cup flour all-purpose
- 1 tsp powder baking
- 1 egg large
- 3 Tbsp of milk
- 3 Tbsp of sugar
- 2 Tbsp oil neutral-flavored

***For Corn & Cheese Cake*:**

- ½ cup flour all-purpose
- 1 tsp powder baking
- 1 egg large
- 3 Tbsp of milk
- 4 Tbsp of sugar
- 1 Tbsp oil neutral-flavored
- ¼ cup canned corn or frozen
- ¼ cup cheese shredded

For Double Chocolate Steamed Cake:

- ½ cup flour all-purpose
- 1 tsp powder baking
- 1 & ½ Tbsp cocoa powder unsweetened
- 1 egg large
- 3 Tbsp of milk
- 3 Tbsp sugar
- 3 Tbsp oil neutral-flavored
- 3 Tbsp chips chocolate

NUTRITION

Calories 467 Kcal | fat 21 g | Carbohydrate 59 g | Protein 13 g

INSTRUCTIONS

1. To avoid condensation, place a kitchen towel on the lid. Put ½ inch of water in the bottom of a big frying pan. Take a pan & cover it with a lid, then bring water to a boil. If you don't have a pressure cooker, you may use a conventional steamer, but cooking time would take a little longer.

FOR BASIC STEAMED CAKE

2. Assemble everything you'll need. 4 6-oz ramekins & cupcake liners are also required for this recipe.
3. Whisk the all-purpose flour & baking powder together in a medium bowl until thoroughly combined.
4. The egg, milk, oil, and sugar should be mixed and dissolved inside a small bowl.
5. Whisk the egg yolks and flour together in a separate bowl until barely blended and smooth. Don't combine too much.

6. Divide your batter among the glass ramekins lined with cupcake liners.

7. Take out the ramekins from the boiling water, cover them with a lid, and cook for 8 minutes on the lowest setting.

8. When a skewer poked into one of the cakes comes out clean, they're done.

9. Remove your ramekins from the oven and place them on a wire rack to cool. Serve hot or cold, depending on your preference.

FOR CORN & CHEESE CAKE

10. Whisk the all-purpose flour & baking powder together in a large bowl until thoroughly combined.

11. The sugar, egg, milk, and oil should all be whisked together in a medium bowl until well blended and the sugar is dissolved.

12. Whisk the egg yolks and flour together in a separate bowl until barely blended and smooth. Don't over-mix the ingredients.

13. Mix in the corn and cheese until they're evenly distributed. Divide the batter among the glass ramekins lined with a cupcake liner.

14. Cook your glass ramekins for around 12-13 minutes in a pot of boiling water, with the lids on the lowest heat setting. When a skewer poked into one of the cakes comes out clean, they're done.

15. Remove your ramekins from the pan and allow them to cool on the wire rack when the heat has been turned off. Serve at room temperature or hotter if desired.

16. For Double Chocolate Steamed Cake

17. Mix flour, baking powder, cocoa powder, and salt in a small bowl and whisk to combine.

18. The sugar, egg, milk, and oil should all be whisked together in a medium bowl until well blended and the sugar is dissolved.

19. Whisk the egg yolks and flour together in a separate bowl until barely blended and smooth. Don't over-mix the ingredients.

20. Mix in the chocolate chunks until they're evenly distributed. Divide the batter among the glass ramekins lined with a cupcake liner.

21. Cook ramekins for around 8 minutes at low heat with the lids on a pot of boiling water. When a skewer poked into one of the cakes comes out clean, they're done. Remove your ramekins from the pan and allow them to cool on the wire rack when the heat has been turned off. Serve at room temperature or hotter if desired.

CONCLUSION

Eating food in bento boxes is more than just eating sparse aliments in a box.
It's a tradition, a tidy way of nurturing ourself, and a healthier way to think about food. Especially if you have children, they will be amused to eat their "food in a box", especially if you give it a try to simulate their favorite anime's characters, and no, you don't need to be an artist. It can actually become a nice moment to share a funny activity with your kids, making them experience the process of creating what they will then eat. I promise they will look forward to their lunch time, just as I was looking forward to my mum's homemade bento.
Be creative and dare to mix recipes, tastes and colors at your will. Putting simplicity and creativity back into cooking will pay big dividends.
I really hope that this joinery into Japanese cuisine has contributed to enrich and maybe change your eating habits. I'm sure you have found your go-to recipes among the many proposed here.
If you have found my book of any value I'd be glad you could share a review in the website you purchased it from.

Made in United States
Troutdale, OR
12/01/2023

15205317R00077